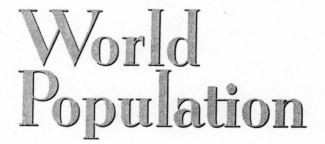
World Population

Challenges for the 21st Century

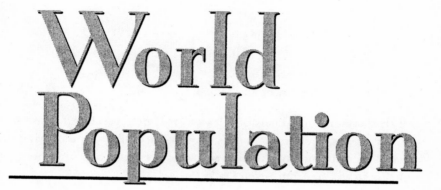

World Population

Challenges for the 21st Century

LEON F. BOUVIER
JANE T. BERTRAND

SEVEN LOCKS PRESS

Santa Ana, California
Minneapolis, Minnesota
Washington D.C.

Manufactured in the United States of America.

Seven Locks Press
P.O. Box 25689
Santa Ana, CA 92799
(800) 354-5348

Bouvier, Leon F.
    World population : challenges for the 21st century / Leon F.
Bouvier, Jane T. Bertrand.
        p.   cm.
    Includes biliographical references and index.
    ISBN 0-929765-66-4
    1. Population. 2. Overpopulation. 3. Population forecasting.
I. Bertrand, Jane T.   II. Title.
HB871.B589   1999
304.6—dc21   99-28339
                                                        CIP

Contents

v

List of Tables and Figures

Acknowledgments

In preparing this book, the authors received useful and valuable advice from a number of sources. Leon Bouvier wishes to offer his sincere thanks to his friend and colleague Lindsey Grant for his advice and encouragement in developing the outline for this book. Grant and Bouvier are the co-authors of *How Many Americans* (Sierra Club Books, 1994), and in a sense, the present book is an outgrowth of that one, though much broader in scope.

Leon Bouvier also wishes to thank his friend of many years, Dr. John Tanton. John has long been interested in the issues discussed in this book, and his encouragement has been wonderful through the years. Thank you, John. Thanks also go to the staff of Social Contract for their excellent cooperation in completing this book.

Jane Bertrand wishes to acknowledge the assistance of three colleagues who reviewed parts of her chapters: Steven Sinding of the Rockefeller Foundation, Karen Stanecki of the Bureau of the Census, and Deborah Billings of IPAS. In addition, she extends thanks to a number of graduate students at Tulane University who assisted in the background research for this book: Kim Longfield, Kama Garrison, Jessica Gipson, Alisa Jenny, M. Celeste Marin, and Mary Yetto.

Elaine Dawson did all the word processing necessary to put the manuscript into final shape. Her expertise and cooperation are both deeply appreciated.

A very special thank you goes to the donor who wishes to remain anonymous for supporting this project. The donor was not only very generous but also patient with us as we tried to meet deadlines. Thank you so much.

We thank Sharon Goldinger, our editor at Seven Locks Press. She and her associates were extremely helpful and cooperative as we labored together preparing the final draft.

Finally, we thank Jim Riordan, publisher of Seven Locks Press, for his encouragement, patience, and willingness to publish our research.

It goes without saying, of course, that the final product reflects our opinions solely and does not necessarily reflect those of the donor, the publisher, or the many friends who were kind enough to offer suggestions.

PART I

Current and Future Demographic Trends

CHAPTER 1

Introduction

As we approach the onset of the new millennium, it is increasingly clear that the demographic patterns that have been taking place and presumably will continue to do so for the foreseeable future will present humankind with enormous challenges—both direct and indirect. Indeed, the soon-to-end 20th century has witnessed the greatest demographic shifts in history.

There can be little doubt that these demographic shifts have been at the heart of the many other changes that have happened to humankind in the 20th century. This invites the question, What about the 21st century? Will the demographic patterns in fertility, mortality, and migration continue at their present rates, or will radical shifts take place? And what will the answers mean for humankind?

In this book we will examine these patterns of demographic behavior and then look at their potential impact on human societies in the 21st century. We should also make it clear that while we will discuss the entire world, the United States—being the nation to which many people desire to migrate—will receive special attention.

First, we will look at sheer population growth—recent, current, and future. This issue has been discussed in many forums. The United Nations (UN) recently published its latest world population projections,[1] but much more research is needed on this problem. Most UN as well as World Bank calculations project an end to growth in that all countries are assumed to eventually reach replacement-level fertility or very close to it. This projection is quite optimistic, at least in the short run. Furthermore, even where family planning programs are hailed as great successes, such as in Mexico and Bangladesh, the problem of growth remains unsolved. For example, in Mexico, even if the fertility rate fell from 3.1 as it is today (in 1998) to 2.1 by 2020, its population would still increase from 91 million to 154 million by 2050 and would still be growing. Numerous studies have shown that, while it is a fairly straightforward process for the fertility of a developing country to fall from 6 or 7 to 4 births per woman, it is extremely difficult for that fertility rate to continue falling to 2 births per woman, and 2 births per woman must be the goal of humankind if we are to reach an end to growth.[2]

Between 1900 and 2000, world population will have increased from about 1.7 billion to over 6 billion. How much will it grow between 2000 and 2050? We don't know, although the United Nations' latest medium projection suggests a population just over 9.3 billion by then, with future growth anticipated. This rapid growth is a subject that must be investigated and one for which possible alternative paths offered.

World population growth is not randomly distributed over the planet. Since about 1920, growth in the less developed countries has far surpassed that in the industrialized nations. Between 1995 and 2050, developed countries are projected to grow by only 50 million people, while poorer regions could grow by 2.3 billion. Even with successful family planning programs, countries such as Mexico, India, Bangladesh, and others will exhibit enormous growth over the next century. Reductions to, say, 4 births per woman will not suffice. The world promises to be a more habitable place only if fertility falls even more.

On the other hand, many of the richer countries are faced with a new demographic challenge—how to avoid demographic suicide (as opposed to demographic genocide). Many cultures, or "civilizations," to borrow from historian Samuel Huntington's recent work, have disappeared throughout history.[3] Most such occurrences resulted from wars against in-migrating hordes; high mortality accounted for the disappearance. In some cases, the group under attack simply moved on and became assimilated by its neighbors; high levels of out-migration accounted for that disappearance. But to the best of our knowledge, no society has ever "voluntarily" disappeared from the face of the earth through low fertility.

What are the current and future prospects of countries where fertility has been well below replacement level for some time and shows no indication of increasing to replacement level? In Germany, for example, the year 2000 population of about 82 million will fall to 69 million by 2050, even if fertility rises from its current low 1.3 births per woman to 1.9 and if there is no immigration. Much has been written about exponential growth (2, 4, 8, 16, 32 . . .), but little has been written about exponential decline (100, 50, 25, 12.5, 6.25 . . .). Again citing Germany, in 2050 its "growth rate" would be −0.7 percent. This means that the population would be reduced by half every 70 years should such a rate be maintained. This would result in fewer children being born and eventually becoming future parents. As is the case for exponential growth and decline, much has been written about the momentum for population growth; little, if anything, has been written about momentum for population decline. Upward and downward momentums work in the same way except that in downward momentum, the most dramatic change occurs in the first period. Thus, the momentum for decline is present and powerful in those countries where fertility remains well below replacement level for a fairly long period, as it has in Germany and numerous other European and erstwhile Union of Soviet Socialist Republics (USSR) nations.

We also must consider the awesome possibilities of increased mortality in some parts of the world. This is already occurring in portions of Africa due to AIDS (acquired immune deficiency syndrome), malaria, and other debilitating diseases, as well as war. Negative population growth is also beginning to take place in Russia through a combination of incredibly low fertility and decreasing life expectancy.

A second pattern to be discussed concentrates on international migration—its past, present, and possible future directions. This flows directly from the discussion of declining population in many rich countries and the rapid growth in most poor countries. This issue is fraught with difficulties, given the possibility for racist overtones, but it must be addressed. If the rich countries are about to lose population and the poor countries' populations are increasing far too rapidly, the solution seems obvious: send millions of people from the poor to the rich regions of the world to re-establish demographic balance! This suggestion has recently received considerable attention in the world of fiction—in particular, in the renewed interest in Jean Raspail's *The Camp of Saints* and the British Broadcasting Corporation–produced film *The March*. In nonfiction, the *Atlantic Monthly* has published important articles at least tangentially related to this demographic issue. While these papers, fiction or nonfiction, express concern with massive population growth in the less developed regions, little if any attention is ever given to the equally important demographic phenomenon of declining population in some industrialized nations.

Most advanced nations, particularly in Europe and Japan, cannot afford to continue to lose population for many more decades. Neither can they grow much more. Countries such as France, Germany, and Japan are at the limits of their carrying capacities. In our view, the solution is not to increase fertility to above replacement in the rich countries, as that would simply contribute to increased world population. Rather, continued low, near-replacement fertility; very limited and selective immigration; and increased life expectancy should be encouraged in those rich countries so as to achieve zero population growth at a level agreed upon to be economically sound.

Together, these demographic patterns lead to perhaps the most controversial issue of all—the cultural adaptation of newcomers in these host societies where fertility is very low, which is our third point. The issue has been discussed in some depth in the United States, Canada, and Australia, where fertility is not as low as in Europe and Japan. The issue is far from settled as the assimilationists argue with the pluralists as to the better path for these nations to follow.

The issue is even more volatile in Europe and perhaps will be soon in Japan. Countries such as France, Italy, and Japan are far more homogeneous than newer nations such as the United States. How are newcomers to adapt to their new societies, especially as their share of the population increases? Countries such as Germany (and others) may have to accept selected newcomers from poorer regions and help them assimilate into a changing German (or other country's) culture. In other words, Europe and Japan might have to follow the example of the United States insofar as immigrants are concerned.

We will select certain countries as models for the study—Germany, Japan, and the United States as typical "receiving" countries and Mexico, Turkey, and the Philippines as typical "sending" countries. Emphasis will be on the United States. For example, what will happen to immigration if population growth continues unabated in Central America, Asia, and Africa? It is in the best interests of all, including

Americans, for fertility to be drastically reduced in all areas where it is above replacement.

Our conclusions for planet Earth in the 21st century are quite dramatic. First, population growth will, we hope, stop well under 10 billion based on persistent efforts to achieve lower fertility. Second, Western civilization (or more specifically, European civilization) as we now know it will probably be drastically altered during the next century. We do not see this as a doomsday scenario. Most civilizations make their contributions and then disappear to be replaced by other civilizations. More realistically, they *converge* with other civilizations. It is quite possible that the 21st century will be the "Pacific century," notwithstanding Asia's recent economic problems.

In that situation, the United States will be ideally situated between the "old" (i.e., Europe) and the "new" (i.e., Asia), providing the United States does not increase its population too much through immigration, making it geographically and culturally more pluribus (many) than unum (one). Under ideal conditions—social, economical, and cultural—the 21st century could indeed be not only the Pacific century but the American century as well.

Some cultural and economic convergence may be needed in the 21st century. As European civilization recedes in importance, it is vital that the change be smooth and that European civilization bequeath its very best qualities (and they are myriad) to the next leading world civilizations. This can occur only if the rich countries of Europe and Japan alter their ethnic compositions very gradually rather than being overwhelmed by millions coming out of the south, as in Raspail's fictional *Camp of Saints*.[4]

What is particularly obvious as we look at the next century is that the demographic changes of the 20th century will continue and will have staggering political and social consequences in the 21st century. These are indeed the greatest challenges facing humankind.

CHAPTER 2

A Brief History of Human Population

Between 1900 and 2000, world population will increase from about 1.7 billion to over 6 billion. In the life of this book's senior author, the world population has tripled. When one realizes that the first billion was not reached until almost 1850, biologist Joel Cohen's recent comment, "Globally, present population growth vastly outpaces past population growth,"[5] is, in fact, an understatement. To put it in another way, "The human species may be more than 100,000 years old but the bulk of its numerical growth has come in just the last few decades: 2.6 billion of today's 5.7 billion people have been born since 1960."[6]

Consider that in this century, the developing nations have surpassed the industrialized nations in population. Consider that immigration has reached unheard-of proportions. Consider too the changes in mortality: life expectancy is rising almost everywhere, in some places at enormous rates, but AIDS, malaria, and other environmentally related diseases haunt us all. The planet reached its second billion in about 1930. It could possibly surpass 8 billion in 2030, should current demographic conditions prevail.

These massive demographic shifts have been at the heart of many other changes in the 20th century. For example, in his recent book, *At a Century's Ending*, George Kennan writes: "[A]ccount must be taken of two developments of the past century, very recent ones in fact, that impose strains on international organizations. . . . These are the problems of global environmental deterioration and overpopulation."[7]

Earlier, Kennan expressed concern for the U.S. population: "This [optimal] balance, in the case of the United States, would seem to me to have been surpassed when the American population reached, at a very maximum, two hundred million people and perhaps a good deal less."[8]

Population increases in the United States have been even more remarkable as immigration has contributed to that growth. From 4 million at the first census in 1790, the population reached 76 million in 1900 and now surpasses 260 million. In the lifetime of most U.S. citizens, the population has at least doubled, if not tripled.

For most of history, birth and death rates were both very high, resulting in very slow growth. Beginning in the 19th century, mortality began to fall rather rapidly in what are now the developed countries (i.e., Europe and its former colonies, including the United States, as well as Japan). Fertility, however, remained high for quite a few decades before beginning a long-term decline that continues to this day (the "baby boom" being an exception). As a result, population growth increased tremendously in these countries.

However, the less developed regions (e.g., Africa, Latin America, and most of Asia) continued to have both high birth and high death rates until the middle of the 20th century. Then mortality began to fall, in some cases very rapidly. Slow growth was followed by very rapid growth (sometimes over 3 percent per year) in recent decades as fertility remained high in most such countries and mortality fell. Thus, while population growth is relatively low (and even negative) in developed countries, it remains high in most developing nations (see figure 2.1).[9]

By the mid-1990s, 80 percent (4.7 billion) of the world's population inhabited the less developed regions, while only 20 percent (1.2 billion) lived in the developed countries (see figure 2.2). Just one century ago, the pattern was almost reversed, with a majority of Earth's inhabitants residing in its more developed countries. The conclusion is obvious: not only has population growth been enormous in the 20th century, it has also led to a complete reversal of population distribution with the poorer regions gaining and surpassing the richer sections in the process.

Age composition, too, has a tremendous impact on many facets of social life—from schools to the labor force to retirement. The "age" of

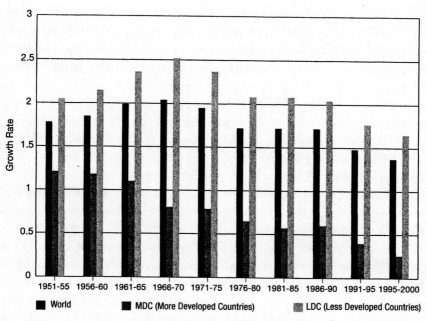

Source: *United Nations World Population Prospects: The 1996 Revision.*

Figure 2.1—MDC and LOC Growth Rates, 1950–2000

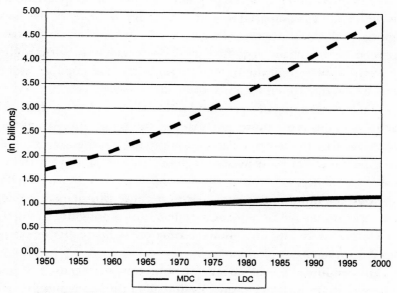

Source: *United Nations World Population Prospects: The 1996 Revision.*

Figure 2.2—Population of MDC and LDC, 1950–2000

a nation is almost as important as its population size.[10] As a rule, developed countries that normally exhibit low fertility and mortality rates are "older" than less developed nations where fertility is high and mortality may or may not be declining. For example, in Sweden, there are as many "elderly" as there are persons under age 15. On the other hand, in Nigeria, 45 percent of the population is under 15 and only 3 percent are "elderly." This distribution is typical of developing nations.

The world population as a whole is aging. The proportion under age 15 has fallen from 38 percent in 1965 to 32 percent in 1998. However, the number of young people has grown from 1.2 billion to 1.9 billion. At the other end of the age spectrum, the population 65 and over increased from 178 million in 1965 to 350 million in 1998. Its share rose from 5.3 to 7.0 percent.

Another matter to consider is "population momentum." In a young population, even if couples were to lower their fertility, births would remain high for some time since the number of young people marrying would be large because of previously high fertility. Many women would be "available" to have two or three children. Thus, the number of births would not fall as rapidly as expected despite a significant decline in the fertility rate.

In 1998, 35 percent of the population in less developed countries was under age 15 compared to only 19 percent in the more developed regions. In the latter, 14 percent were age 65 or over compared to only 5 percent in the former regions.[11] Thus, even if all women throughout the world were to limit themselves to two births, the population share living in less developed sections would still increase.

What causes aging of a population? Many would answer that reduction in mortality is the cause. Surprisingly, this is not true. Ansley Coale points out that the average age of a population is the average age of living persons, not their average age at death.[12] Moreover, reduced mortality has increased the number of young persons more than it has increased the number of older persons because typical improvements in health and medicine reduce mortality more among the young than among the old. In other words, the reduction in the death rate has produced a younger population.

This finding is particularly relevant to our investigation of population trends in the 21st century. Even if all of the women in the world had only two children, population would still increase for quite some time simply because of the momentum for growth present in a young population. Declining mortality in the poorer countries means more young people survive to adulthood and have children. In a sense, it contributes to a "baby boom," though with different causes (a decline in infant and childhood mortality) than the baby boom in the United States and elsewhere after World War II (which was due to a fertility increase).

The racial composition of the planet is also changing and will continue to do so. We cannot assume that a country is all white or all black. Furthermore, relatively accurate numbers are not available. But we do know that in the United States the majority Anglo population is gradually losing its lead. In California, for example, among Anglos, Hispanics, Asians, and African Americans, we find that there is no majority. This is quite a shift from just 20 years ago when Anglos clearly dominated the population of the state. It is anticipated that by about 2030, there will be no majority population in the United States. All Americans will be minorities.

Worldwide, nonwhites will continue to increase their share of the population. For now, we can look at each region of the world, bearing in mind our caveat about not assuming that all residents of a particular nation are necessarily of a certain race. According to the Population Reference Bureau, residents of the Asian continent comprise 60.8 percent of all of Earth's inhabitants,[13] followed by Africans (12.9 percent), Europeans (12.3 percent), Latin Americans and Caribbeans (8.4 percent), North Americans (i.e., residents of the United States and Canada) (5.1 percent), and Oceanians (0.5 percent). Table 2.1 below gives the actual numbers as of 1998.

While not necessarily racial in nature, religious shifts are occurring as well. For example, Muslims now represent 18 percent of the world's population, compared to 13 percent for those in Western religions. The Muslim population may well increase in the future to perhaps 20 percent in 2000 and 30 percent by 2025, while that of Western religions will decline.[14]

It is clear that Asians now dominate the world population. Whites are a falling minority. In summary, combined rapid population growth, changing age composition, altered population distribution,

REGION	NUMBER (IN MILLIONS)	PERCENT
Asia	3,604	60.8
Africa	763	12.9
Europe	728	12.3
Latin America and Caribbean	500	8.4
North America	301	5.1
Oceania	30	0.5

Table 2.1—Population of the World by Region, 1998
Source: *1998 World Population Data Sheet* (Washington, D.C.: Population Reference Bureau, 1998).

and significant racial changes have been the principal demographic factors that faced the planet in the 20th century. The actions of billions of people, whether they increased or decreased fertility and/or mortality, whether they migrated or not, changed the face of planet Earth more so than in any previous century. Let us now consider what is likely to happen in the 21st century.

CHAPTER 3

World Population in the 21st Century

Recent demographic trends can be described without exaggeration as revolutionary, a virtual discontinuity with all of human history. Consider, for example, the astonishing fact that although the human species originated perhaps 150,000 years ago, most of its growth in numbers has occurred in the last 40 years. When we realize that it was not until about 1850 that world population reached its first billion and that it is now over 6 billion, it becomes altogether clear that for most of the time *Homo sapiens* has been on this planet, growth has been infinitesimal. The projections discussed here strongly suggest that such a demographic balance will necessarily take place again in the not-too-distant future as population approaches the ultimate carrying capacity of the planet. According to the 1994 *State of the World* report from the World Watch Institute, slowed growth in world food supplies suggests that the planet's biological limits may have been reached already.

What do the numbers tell us? Currently, we are adding 95 million people to the world population every year. In effect, we add one Mexico every year. By comparison, 25 million were added annually during the 1940s and 70 million per year in the 1960s.

According to the population projections from the United Nations Population Division (*1998 Revisions of the World Population Projections*), another billion people will be added to the world's population during the 1990s, which will surpass 6 billion in 2000. By 2050, the world population will likely be about 9 billion. Even under the highly unlikely "low" fertility series, which assumes an eventual world fertility rate of 1.6 live births per woman, the population would surpass 7.3 billion by the year 2050.[15] Table 3.1 illustrates the population growth under the UN high, medium, and low series. Also included is the constant series, which assumes no change in fertility over time. Instant replacement, taken from an earlier UN publication, shows what would occur if fertility fell to replacement everywhere in 1990—an obviously impossible situation.

If there were no changes in fertility after 1990, the world's population would reach an incredible 15 *billion* in 2050 and continue to grow at a rate of 2.1 percent per year. That means a doubling of the population every 35 years. Should that rate be maintained, by 2100 the population of the world would surpass 40 billion! Such a colossal number is not being predicted by anyone; however, it does answer the question, What would happen if current patterns of fertility remained constant? The other hypothetical model (instant replacement) answers the question, What if replacement fertility had occurred in 1990 throughout the world and remained constant thereafter? Even under such impossible assumptions, numbers would still increase, reaching 7 billion by 2025 and 8 billion by 2100, before leveling off at about 8.4 billion in 2150. This is an excellent example of population momentum, discussed earlier.

YEAR	MEDIUM	HIGH	LOW	INSTANT REPLACEMENT	CONSTANT
2000	6,091	6,123	6,062	5,792	6,141
2025	8,039	8,581	7,474	7,069	9,212
2050	9,367	11,156	7,662	7,697	14,941

Table 3.1—Projected Population of the World, 2000-2050 (in millions)
Source: United Nations, *World Population Prospects: The 1996 Revision.*

Turning to the more realistic 1998 projections, the "medium" series is often referred to as the most likely future scenario. Under this series, world population would reach almost 9 billion by 2050 and would still be growing, albeit at a low rate (0.45). Recall, however, that this assumes all regions will reach replacement fertility at some time in the future. In Africa, for example, replacement is assumed to occur by 2030–2035 according to the medium projection, quite an optimistic assumption.

World population will continue to grow rapidly, even in the short-term future. Relying on the new and very conservative medium UN projection, the total population by 2025 may reach 8 billion.[16] This increase will take place despite the fact that the annual growth rate is projected to decline from 1.7 percent to only 1 percent by 2025. If we turn to the high projection, which may be more realistic, world population could reach 8.5 billion by 2025 and 11.1 billion in 2050.

But how large can population grow? Or, to borrow from Joel Cohen's text, "How many people can the earth support?" Unfortunately, Cohen never tells us his opinion, but he does enumerate the variables that must be considered before arriving at an answer. For example, at what standard of living? That of the United States, France, or the Democratic Republic of the Congo (formerly Zaire)? He does conclude, however, the following:

> The human population of the earth now travels in the zone when a substantial fraction of scholars have estimated upper limits on human population size. These estimates are no better than present understanding of humankind's cultural, economic, and environmental choices and constraints. Nevertheless, the possibility must be considered seriously that the number of people on the Earth has reached, or will reach within half a century, the maximum number the Earth can support in modes of life that we and our children and their children will choose to want.[17]

It may seem contradictory to project such momentous increases while the growth rate itself is falling. Three factors account for this apparent anomaly. First, the population itself is expanding. Even though the growth rate may be falling, it is based on an ever-growing population. Second, infant and child mortality rates have fallen rapidly in many developing countries over the past few decades. As noted earlier, this has resulted in a sort of "baby boom" attributable not to higher fertility but to lower mortality. This baby boom has contributed to the third factor. In any young population, a built-in momentum for growth is present. Looking at the world, and particularly the developing regions, the number of young people is enormous, proportionally speaking (in part because of falling infant and child mortality). Even if these people decide to lower their fertility, the number of births will increase because more and more women of reproductive age are available to have children. This explains the hypothetical projection that indicated that even if fertility had reached the replacement level in 1990, world population would still grow to 8.4 billion before leveling off—yet another example of population momentum. In demographic terms, shutting off the valve instantly is simply not possible.

The conclusion is apparent. Despite recent declines in fertility, rapid population growth is in store for the planet for the foreseeable future. However, different regions and countries will exhibit vastly different demographic scenarios. Let us briefly summarize these scenarios.

Regional Scenarios

Of the 90 million people added to the world population each year during the 1990s, only 8 million were added each year in the more developed regions. In other words, about 80 percent of the world's population, or 4.7 billion people, live in the less developed regions. The remaining 20 percent (1.2 billion people) reside in the more developed regions. There the average annual growth rate is a mere 0.3 percent, compared to 1.9 percent for the less developed regions.

Relying solely on the UN medium-level projection, the population of the more developed regions may increase by 48 million between 1995 and 2025. The population of the less developed regions could increase by 2.3 billion. Over this 30-year period, practically all of the world population increase will occur in the poorer regions. By 2025, 85 percent of the world's people will live in its poorer regions.

The projected variations in growth will result in Europe's and Russia's share of the world population falling from 13 percent to 8.7 percent by 2025. North America will see its proportion fall from 5.2 percent to about 4.5 percent. Europe's population is expected to increase by only about 3 million, reaching 701 million in 2025. North America's population will grow by about 73 million, reaching 369 million.

Such small increases will be dwarfed by those expected in the rest of the world. Africa's share of the world population could approach 19 percent by 2025, at which time its numbers could approach 1.5 billion—double its present size. The countries of Latin America should remain at about 8.5 percent of the world population over the next 30 years; however, actual numerical size will grow from 470 million to 689 million. Asia's share should remain at about 60 percent, but its actual population may grow from 3.4 billion in 1995 to 4.8 billion in 2025 (see figure 3.1).

Thus far, we have limited our discussion to fertility and mortality as contributing factors to population growth. With such a disparity in growth rates, we must ask, "What about immigration?" with immigration occurring primarily from poorer to richer nations. (This topic will be discussed in more detail in chapter 4.) To illustrate the dramatic

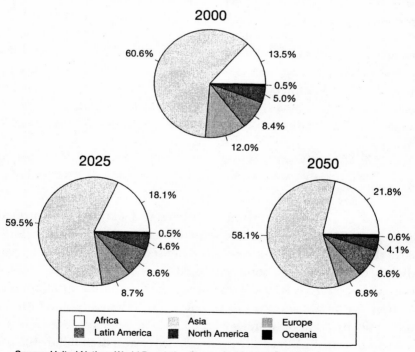

Source: *United Nations World Population Prospects: The 1996 Revision.*

Figure 3.1—Population by Regions, 2000, 2025, 2050

demographic changes expected in sending and receiving countries, table 3.2 shows a few typical countries and their UN medium-level projections from 1995 to 2050 and includes 1960 figures to highlight the differences in population growth between the developing and developed nations.

COUNTRY	1960	1995	2000	2010	2025	2050
France	45,684	58,104	59,061	59,944	60,393	59,883
Germany	72,673	81,594	82,688	82,483	80,877	73,303
Italy	50,200	57,204	57,194	55,828	53,237	41,197
United Kingdom	52,372	58,079	58,336	58,727	59,535	56,667
United States	180,671	267,115	277,325	298,885	332,481	349,318
Canada	17,909	29,402	30,678	33,010	36,385	42,311
Japan	94,096	125,068	126,428	127,044	121,348	104,921
Australia	10,315	17,866	18,838	20,853	23,931	25,761
Algeria	10,800	28,109	31,599	38,636	47,322	57,731
Nigeria	42,305	111,721	128,786	168,369	238,397	244,311
Pakistan	49,955	136,257	156,007	200,621	268,904	345,484
Philippines	27,561	67,839	75,037	88,813	105,194	130,893
Turkey	27,509	60,838	65,732	74,624	85,791	100,664
Haiti	3,804	7,124	7,817	9,416	12,513	15,174
Mexico	36,530	91,145	98,881	112,891	130,196	146,645

Table 3.2—Selected Country Populations, 1960 and 1995–2050 (in thousands)
Source: United Nations, *World Population Prospects: The 1996 Revision;* for 2050, United Nations, *The 1998 Revision.*

Most European receiving countries will exhibit little growth between 1995 and 2025. Italy's population may actually be smaller in 2025 than it was in 1995. Other European receiving countries will grow slightly only because of some immigration. The fertility level in most European countries is so low that in the absence of immigration, population size would soon begin to fall. Japan's demographic future is very similar to that of western Europe, and its population is expected to grow only from 125 to 127 million by 2010 and then fall to 105 million by 2050. These very slow growth patterns are simply an extension of the past few decades. Germany's population (East and West Germany combined) was almost 73 million in 1960; that of Italy surpassed 50 million. Growth since 1960 has been extremely slow in Europe as well as in Japan.

This reflects not only low fertility but what could be called "reverse momentum"—the mirror image of growth momentum. For example, if women average 1.5 births for a generation, then the next generation will have a shortage of adult marriage-age women, and the population will keep falling even if these women have, say, two children on average. Only in the United States, Canada, and Australia is growth expected to be fairly robust in the first quarter of the 21st century, and again this is due primarily to immigration. Indeed, the Census Bureau projects that the United States will have a population of well over 300 million before the middle of the 21st century.

Growth among selected typical sending countries provides a vastly different picture. Nigeria's population, for example, is expected to grow to 244 million by 2050. Haiti's 1960 population of 3.8 million will quadruple to 15.1 million by 2050. The Mexican population could reach 146 million, up from 91 million in 1995. Such growth could accelerate massive out-migration in a country such as Haiti, where a population of 15 million inhabitants is almost incomprehensible. Past growth in these countries has been extremely rapid. Nigeria's population increased from 42 million in 1960 to 111 million in 1995, Mexico's from 37 to 91 million, Turkey's from 28 to 61 million.

The world's population will grow for the foreseeable future. Adding almost 100 million people annually is now commonplace. Furthermore, this growth will take place primarily in those regions that can least support it. By 2025, Turkey's population will be greater than Germany's. Algeria's population will be fast approaching that of France and will surpass it soon after 2050. This is in marked contrast to 1960, when there were more than four times as many French as there were Algerians. By 2025, population growth will still be high in the poorer countries, while growth will have nearly ended in the richer countries. Indeed, in some countries the population will be falling. It should be added that the newest UN revisions (1998), which take AIDS into account, project considerably smaller populations in many African countries (and elsewhere) than had been projected in the 1996 revision. For example, Nigeria's population in 2050, under the 1998 revision (which includes deaths estimated to be attributable to

AIDS), is projected at 244 million compared to 338 million under the 1996 revision.

Can the Third World support such growth? How can the industrialized nations assist their developing country counterparts in coping with such growth? Can lower fertility be achieved, or will it be necessary to accept millions of immigrants to restore some sort of balance to the world population? The answers to these questions will help determine what kind of a world humans will be living in, in the 21st century.

Age Scenario

Another aspect of shifts in demographic behavior exists that may be as serious as migration in some instances. We are referring to changes in age composition. The world population is aging (see figure 3.2). "Demographers call the 80-plus group the 'oldest old' and it is one of the fastest growing population segments around the world."[18] The future will see further aging of the world population, though all age groups will grow. By 2025, the number of children under age 15 will surpass 2.5 billion, representing 24.3 percent of the world's people. The elderly population will reach 824 million and comprise 10 percent of the total. Nicholas Kristoff writes:

> Worldwide, the great comet of boomers is beginning to cross the 50-year milestone . . . and the result will be to create a global society that is by far the oldest in the history of the world. This aging process will be one of the dominant trends over the coming decades in the industrialized world—and, for different reasons, in the Third World as well—reshaping societies across the globe.[19]

That leaves the so-called active population, those between the ages of 15 and 65. Their number will increase substantially, from 3.2 billion in 1990 to 5.5 billion in 2025. By that year, there will be as many people in their active ages as there are people in the world today! If we assume that about 60 percent of the people in the active years are in the work force, that means that the work force will grow from about 1.9 billion in 1990 to 3.3 billion in 2025—a gain of 1.4 billion individuals in a mere 35 years.

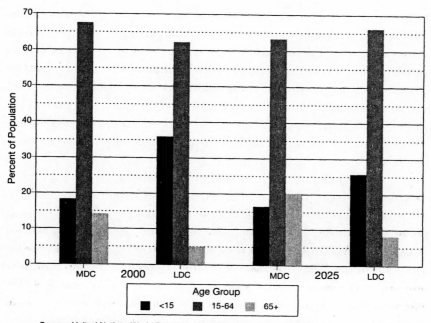

Figure 3.2—Population by Age Group, MDC and LDC, 2000 and 2025

Source: *United Nations World Population Prospects: The 1996 Revision.*

In the developing countries, 36 percent of the population (1.5 billion) is under 15 years of age. In East, Middle, and West Africa, about 40 percent of the population is under 15, and this group numbers 281 million. In East Asia, the proportion of youth is 26 percent, but this segment numbers 366 million. More growth is foreseen for the future. By 2025, the almost 1.9 billion children under 15 will represent 26 percent of the population of developing nations.

One of the little-discussed problems facing these nations in the future is the increasing size of their elderly populations. From 182 million in 1990, the number of elderly will soar to 567 million 35 years later. Their proportion of the population will double from 4 to 8 percent. Few developing countries are preparing themselves for the onslaught of the elderly—the result of high fertility and falling child mortality in previous decades—that will soon be facing them.

The active population is expected to increase rapidly in the near future—from 2.4 billion in 1990 to 4.6 billion in 2025. Of special importance to the future economies of the developing countries is the size of their projected work force. "With 36 percent of the population under 15 years of age, the labor force in the developing world will grow by 38 million a year during the 1990s."[20] Indeed, the United Nations Population Division predicts that "additions to the labor force in developing countries, 732 million over the next 20 years, will exceed the entire 1990 labor force of the industrialized countries of 686 million."[21] This suggests that by 2025, over 2.7 billion people may be in the labor force of the developing regions.

In Mexico alone, a million people enter the work force annually. Despite recent declines in fertility, 38 percent (32 million) of Mexico's population is under age 15. Thus, the potential for continued growth of its labor force is awesome. On the other hand, only 3 million Mexicans are 65 or over, and they comprise less than 4 percent of the population. By 2025, because of falling fertility, youths will still total about 32 million and represent 23 percent of the population. The elderly group will surpass 11.6 million, and its share of the total population will be 9.3 percent. Because of earlier high fertility, the active group between 15 and 65 will almost double from 49 to 94 million, which suggests massive increases in attempts to migrate elsewhere.

Similar distributions are noted in most typical sending countries. Twenty million Turks are under age 15 while only 2.4 million are elderly. Here, too, aging will occur. By 2025 the respective shares of young and old will be 23.2 and 9.3 percent. In the same interval the active population will grow from 33.6 million to 63.4 million—again suggesting accelerated movements of people out of the country.

The examples of Mexico and Turkey are especially relevant since they represent the typical international migration pattern where people from one country tend to migrate to a specific other country: Turkey to Germany, Mexico to the United States, Algeria to France, and so on. These shifts in age composition vividly demonstrate the UN conclusion that "Past rapid growth may well have a decisive effect on current migratory trends as new and larger age cohorts move into the workforce."[22] This statement is even more appropriate for the near future than it is for the present.

In industrialized countries, the proportion of the population age 65 or over is considerably higher than that in developing regions. In

1990, 12 percent of the population of the industrialized nations was 65 or over and numbered 145 million. The under-15 age group numbered 260 million and comprised 21 percent of the population. The proportion that is 65 or over will jump from 12 percent in 1990 to 16 percent in 2010 and 20 percent in 2025. By that time, 7.8 percent of the population in the more developed regions will be over age 75. At the other end of the age scale, the youth population will be slightly smaller in 2025 than it was in 1990—256 million. Young people will comprise 17 percent of the population of these countries, reflecting the impact of continued low fertility.

The all-important active population (between ages 15 and 65) totaled 806 million in 1990. By 2025, that number will have increased to 891 million—a minuscule gain when compared to the 2.2 billion gain in this age group in the developing regions. This translates into about 535 million people in the actual work force of the industrialized countries. In contrast, the labor force in the developing regions will surpass 2.7 billion.

The implications of these shifts in age composition are monumental. Even if there were no differentials in growth, these shifts alone would provide the world with massive challenges. Most pressing will be the job demands of the billions of residents of developing countries. Even in the most optimistic scenario, it appears virtually impossible to provide a sufficient number of jobs for these teeming billions. Utilization of this growing resource calls for adequate flows of capital for investment and technology transfers from the more affluent to the less affluent nations. "Failing that, the combination of large increases in population, . . . excess labor supply over available jobs, rising social and therefore political turbulence, and persistent or worsening inequalities between richer and poorer countries, will inevitably stimulate migration in search of better living conditions."[23]

Most of the world's industrialized nations are faced with a terrible demographically driven dilemma. Let us state it in very lucid terms.

Almost without exception, the world's industrialized nations exhibit below-replacement fertility. (The U.S. fertility is just below replacement at about 2.05.) Without any immigration, these nations will soon begin to lose population if they have not already done so. And what if immigration levels are maintained and possibly increased while fertility remains low? Eventually the immigrants and their descendants would become the majority in the respective host countries. How long it would take to accomplish such a goal depends on the level of fertility of both the native-born and newcomer groups, as well as the level of immigration.

The quandary is difficult indeed: either lose population or lose identity. The dilemma is made all the more difficult when one recalls that while the advanced nations are becoming more technologically sophisticated, the rest of the world is not only growing at incredible rates but also falling further behind technologically. "Between 1950 and today per capita income in the rich countries has almost tripled, while in the poorer countries there has been no improvement."[24] As historian Paul Kennedy has recently commented, "A population explosion on one part of the globe and a technology explosion on the other is not a good recipe for a stable international order."[25] The manner in which the advanced countries of Europe, North America, and Asia settle this demographic dilemma may be the most important policy decision of the 21st century—more important than economic, military, or even environmental decisions.

Nations can be growing, remaining fairly stable, or losing population. With the exception of the three "younger" nations (the United States, Canada, and Australia), growth has been minimal in industrialized nations in recent decades. For all practical purposes, zero and even negative population growth has reached Europe and Japan. Most recent increases in numbers have been due to immigration or the fertility of immigrants rather than natural increases among the native-born residents. The demographic picture in the United States, Canada, and Australia differs somewhat from that in Europe and Japan. Population growth has been greater in those countries in part because of higher levels of immigration but also because of the tremendous momentum for growth emanating from a baby-boom period that lasted much longer than in Europe or Japan.

The U.S. population—150 million in 1950—reached 226 million in 1980 and 250 million by 1990. Similar growth occurred in Canada and Australia. Yet fertility has been below replacement level for the past 20 years in all three countries. Since 1950, perhaps half of all population growth in the United States can be accounted for, directly and indirectly, by immigration. Without immigration the population would not have declined because of the momentum from the baby boom; however, its growth would have been limited.

Mortality declines should also be considered, although they are often neglected. Demographers Samuel Preston and Kevin White calculated what the population of the United States would have been in 1995 if the mortality rates at the turn of the 20th century had not changed. They concluded that there would have been about half as many Americans in today's population—139 million instead of 276 million. Half of the "missing people" would have been absent because one of their parents would not have survived to reproductive age. The other half would have been born but would have died young.[26] No one is advocating a return to high death rates, but bear in mind that any improvements in life expectancy are important contributors to population growth, and if population growth is to be limited, their input should be compensated for by additional declines in either fertility or immigration or both.

Given the population density in Europe and Japan, and given the environmental degradation and resource utilization that result from population growth and higher than average consumption, it seems that any further population growth in Europe and Japan is not only unwarranted but could be detrimental to the quality of life there. As with other industrialized nations, "growing population and industrialization during this century led to atmospheric pollution, contaminated rivers and seas, and a damaged countryside."[27] To be sure, environmental pressure groups emerged and much has been done to alleviate the environmental damage, but any further population growth can only impede such progress. Furthermore, the growing structural shifts in the economy of most advanced countries, together with the progressive reliance on robotics, especially in Japan, suggest that fewer people may suffice in the work force of the future. It could then be argued that some minor reductions in population size might be advantageous and might produce an improved quality of life for the Europeans and Japanese.

Any significant increases in population size in Europe and Japan would be damaging to the respective societies. Most countries are already approaching their maximum carrying capacities. One can hardly visualize 100 million French or Italians! The demographic behavior of the past few decades strongly implies that today's population size is about the most that can be reasonably tolerated in European countries, and this is even more true of Japan.

At first glance, one might think that conditions in the United States, Canada, and Australia are so different that population growth there can continue indefinitely. The United States already has a population of over 260 million, and Americans have by far the largest consumptive appetite of any humans. It has been argued that because of American consumption behavior, the United States is the most overpopulated nation in the world. One hundred million additional Americans could prove disastrous for the environment of the planet. A number of scientists have argued quite convincingly that the population of the United States should be considerably smaller than it is today if Americans are to maintain, even remotely, their present lifestyle.[28] Even in the supposedly underpopulated countries, no growth or even some decline would be advantageous when taking into account not only the economy but the environment, resource depletion, and overall quality of life.

We have discussed the demographic situation in developing countries. Any further growth in such regions is potentially detrimental to many facets of life. Unfortunately, because of the built-in momentum for growth, the population can be expected to increase considerably even if fertility levels are reduced drastically. Therefore, it is vital that continued reductions in fertility occur.

Industrialized Countries without Immigration

The United States, Canada, and Australia may have been built on waves of immigration from various areas of the world. This is not the case in Europe and Japan, however, where homogeneity prevails. The argument that Europe and Japan need immigration to forestall future labor shortages is not a popular one. A UN report points out that unchecked migration "could become the human crisis of our age."[29] In countries such as Germany, France, and the former Yugoslavia, the report continues, people are being rejected by the mainstream of society because they are ethnically, religiously, or culturally different. "There is no doubt that a serious reappraisal of the whole issue of international migration and its implications for national and regional stability is under way."[30] Over 10 years ago, a group of prominent German scholars issued what has become known as the "Heidelberg Manifesto." It "calls for the preservation of Germany's language, culture, and national character against the joint consequences of low native fertility and continued high immigration."[31]

In Japan, there is overwhelming agreement that any immigration must be very limited and temporary. "Tactless remarks by [Japanese] politicians about the social weaknesses of America's multicultural, multiracial population reveal that concerns about preserving 'Japanness' are always likely to outweigh merely utilitarian arguments in favor of increased immigration."[32] In both Australia and Canada (particularly British Columbia), increasing anxiety is being expressed over the rapidly growing Asian presence. In Quebec, the separatist leader blamed immigrants for the failure of separatists to win independence in the 1996 referendum. In Australia, "immigration is never far from the headlines. Support for past immigration flows tends to be almost unanimous but current intakes generate considerable debate."[33] Indeed, "although Asians make up less than 5 percent of Australia's population of 18 million, they account for 40 percent of its current immigrants. Within the next 25 years, according to some projections, they could form a quarter of the country's population."[34] Parliament member Pauline Hanson (recently voted out of office) gained considerable attention with her anti-Asian and anti-Aborigine rhetoric. Hanson's maiden speech to Parliament in September 1996, a call to keep out immigrants, attracted world attention. She claimed Australia will be flooded with Asians by 2040.[35]

In the United States, recent problems of illegal immigration have led to a spreading demand to limit and even reduce immigration levels. A Negative Population Growth (NPG)–sponsored poll in December 1995 found that fully 70 percent of all Americans would prefer that immigration be reduced to less than 300,000 per year. In July 1993, President Clinton proposed new legislation that would, he hoped, drastically curb illegal entries. Yet nothing has been accomplished that would reduce legal immigration, and illegal entries continue at record highs.

In all the typical industrial receiving countries, a strong and some-times growing sentiment to reduce—if not terminate—all international migration is apparent. The dilemma is intensifying. As we have seen in countries such as Germany, many citizens would prefer to put an end to immigration. In France in 1990, Jacques Chirac argued that immigration must be totally stopped. Likewise, former Interior Minister Charles Pasqua stated that "given the seriousness of the situation, the goal we have set is zero immigration."[36] In Germany, former Chancellor Kohl expressed concern about immigration, and the government cut the number of asylum seekers from 430,000 in 1992 to 127,000 in 1998. Somewhat facetiously, the popular magazine *Der Speigel* remarked that "under the sheets Germany is a dying nation." Great Britain reduced the number in its asylum programs from over 20,000 to less than 10,000. "Overall, in the mid-1990s western European countries were moving inexorably toward reducing to a minimum if not totally eliminating immigration from non-European sources."[37]

Others are concerned about "national suicide." In countries such as the United States, some not only argue for continued immigration but claim that increases in those numbers are critical to America's economic progress.[38] Others would like nothing better than to drastically limit or at least have a temporary moratorium on, if not end, such movements across the border. What would be the demographic impact of an end to immigration for these industrialized nations where fertility is already below the level needed to replace the population? Special projections have been prepared for two countries—the United States and Germany—to illustrate what would happen if immigration were to end and fertility were to remain at current levels.

In the United States, even if immigration ended in the year 2000, the population would continue to grow until 2050 when it would peak at 311 million. It would then fall very slowly to 298 million by 2100.[39] According to projections prepared by the Census Bureau, without immigration the nation's population would still surpass 301 million in 2050 and continue to grow very slowly.[40] Of course, if fertility did fall as it did in the 1970s and 1980s, a different picture would emerge. For example, if fertility fell to 1.7 by 2000 and continued to decline to 1.5 by 2050, and if immigration came to an end, the country's population would peak at 291 million in 2020 and drop to 165 million by 2100, still a substantial number.[41]

The demographic picture in Germany differs sharply from that of the United States. Even before unification in October 1990, fertility was low in both East and West Germany. In West Germany in 1985, the total fertility rate (TFR) fell to a worldwide peacetime historical low of 1.27. By 1989, the TFR was about 1.5 in both Germanys. It is currently 1.3, among the lowest in the world. With very low fertility and an old population, a momentum for decline exists just as a momentum for increase is present in a young population. To illustrate this demographic phenomenon we have prepared a set of projections for Germany for the period 2000 to 2075. Assume that fertility will be constant at 1.5, life expectancy will be 79 for males and 85 for females, and no immigration will occur. From an estimated 82 million in 2000, the population would fall to 79 million in 2025, 62 million in 2050, and 47 million by 2075. By that year, the growth rate would be -1.1. At such a rate, the population would be halved about every 70 years.

Populations that exhibit low fertility and no immigration age rapidly. Our two examples are no exception. According to the Census Bureau's "no immigration" scenario, in the United States the proportion of the population age 65 and over would climb from 12 percent today to 23 percent in 2050, and the median age would be 41. By then there would be more elderly persons than children under age 15. Over the period, the number of people between 15 and 65—and thus the labor force—would barely grow. Irrespective of the scenario, however, the nation will age and its elderly population will more than double between now and the middle of the next century. The age shifts in Germany will be even more dramatic. By 2075, 32 percent of all Germans will be 65 or over. Furthermore, the working-age population will gradually decline from 55 million in 2000 to 35 million in 2050 and 27 million in 2075. Thus, the German labor force would be reduced by half if fertility remains at current levels and immigration ceases.

Situations similar to that projected for Germany can be expected for Japan and for the other western European receiving countries. Without some immigration, significant population decline can be expected. In itself, this decline is not necessarily problematic. Smaller populations can contribute to improvements in the quality of life.

However, the built-in momentum for continued population decline must be considered. In addition, the extremely high share of elderly will eventually be a matter of concern. It already is in Japan. "A noted government report, *Japan in the Year 2000*, highlighted population aging, along with internationalization and the maturation of the economy, as the three greatest challenges facing Japan in the 21st century."[42] The 65 and over population in Japan numbered 12 million in 1985 and represented 10.3 percent of the nation's population. By 2025, it is projected to number over 31 million and to represent 23.4 percent of the population.[43] A report from Japan projected that "The latest statistics, released recently, show that Japan's birth rate hit a new low last year (1996), and a government projection now suggests that the population will fall by more than half over the next century. It is forecast to tumble to 55 million in 2100, from 125 million today."[44]

Despite the demands by some people in the receiving countries to limit and even end immigration, it is clear that some such movements should be allowed if countries like Germany and Japan are to survive. The question is, How much immigration can be tolerated? Again, we examine the situation in the United States and Germany as surrogates for the other industrialized receiving countries. The immigration history of the United States is well known. Combined with the low fertility of the resident population—which is not replacing itself—the high level of recent immigration is resulting in a major shift in the racial and ethnic composition of the nation.

Between 1950 and 1988, West Germany gained approximately 7.7 million residents through immigration.[45] Almost 40 percent were of non-German ancestry. Since 1960, there has been a substantial inflow of non-Germans into West Germany. By 1989, some 5 million foreigners who were not of German descent resided in West Germany, accounting for nearly 8 percent of the total population. It is estimated that more than 1 million foreigners have entered Germany alone since it reunited in 1990, with more than 400,000 arriving in each of the past two years.

The "foreign" population (including German-born children of immigrants) is much younger than the ethnic German population. It is also growing through natural increase. Indeed, in 1989 births exceeded deaths among the foreign population by 71,000. Among

Germans, deaths exceeded births by 87,000. This pattern still holds today.

As in the United States, the source of immigration into Germany has shifted in recent years. In the 1970s, Italians and Greeks predominated. By 1990, 33 percent of the non-German population was Turkish, 13 percent was Yugoslav, and 11 percent was Italian. The young age structure and higher fertility among the foreign population, combined with the very low fertility among Germans, means that the foreign segment will continue to grow relative to the larger German base. With any meaningful future immigration, the foreign share of the total population, particularly Turk and Slav, will increase substantially in the early part of the next century.

Given the current fertility in the United States, Germany, and elsewhere, the question becomes, How much immigration is needed for these countries to preserve their economic positions while maintaining a demographic equilibrium and producing no major cultural shocks? In the United States, a continuation of current patterns of fertility and immigration would lead to a population of perhaps 400 million by 2050. Such a size would most certainly result in a deterioration of the quality of life of all Americans; given the rapacious appetites of Americans, it would also seriously jeopardize natural resources throughout the world. Both fertility and immigration should be reduced if the future population is to remain anywhere close to its present size. According to the most recent projections from the Census Bureau, with fertility reduced to 1.8 and net immigration limited to 350,000 annually, the population would peak at 287 million in 2030 and fall to 276 million by 2050.[46] This seems to be an attainable goal. Lower fertility and immigration levels would be even more attractive, and a population under 200 million is both attainable and desirable.

The German situation is quite different, given Germany's very low fertility compared to that of the United States. Heilig and his associates project a population of less than 60 million in 2050 if recent demographic patterns prevail: that is, a TFR of 1.4 and net immigration of 80,000 per year. On the other hand, if fertility increases to 2.1 and immigration rises to 300,000, then the 2050 population of Germany would surpass 95 million and continue to grow.[47] Such a population size would be far too large; however, would a Germany of less than 60 million inhabitants be sufficient economically? One must also bear in mind that the size of the labor force is directly related to the size of the population. If fertility is to remain at its current very low level, then immigration must be increased. If 300,000 individuals were admitted every year, the future population of Germany would be quite stable. It would peak at 88 million in 2020 and fall to 83 million by midcentury, assuming continued low fertility. The former figure would appear to represent a maximum population for Germany in the 21st century.

A similar pattern probably will occur in other west European countries and Japan. The problem facing Japan is particularly perplexing, in large part due to Japan's reluctance to accept immigrants. With its very low fertility and early-retirement customs, Japan's labor force will fall quite rapidly in future years.

> There is, of course, an obvious solution to the changing balance between the size of the Japanese work force and the numbers of elderly dependents: permit the immigration of the tens of thousands of Koreans, Filipinos, Pakistanis, Bangladeshis, and other peoples to gain employment there. Given Japan's exclusive policies as well as its cramped geographical circumstances, this seems highly unlikely.[48]

Declining Homogeneity

The demographic dilemma facing the industrialized receiving nations is especially apparent when data like those just cited for Germany are examined more deeply. First, while some reduction in population size may be acceptable, there is a limit to that decrease. Second, as long as fertility remains at current levels, population size will fall quite rapidly. Third, given such low fertility, this drop can be alleviated only through immigration. Here is the dilemma in stark terms: the result is a culturally and ethnically different Germany, or France, or United States, or even Japan. Using our example of Germany's future population, with annual immigration of 300,000 and continued low fertility, by 2050 one-quarter of the population could consist of post-2000 immigrants and their descendants—all non-Germans. Today close to 10 percent of the German population is foreign. "Already, Germany, Austria, and Hungary feel besieged by refugee families."[49] The United States is well on its way to becoming the first industrialized nation where no single racial group predominates numerically.

An agonizing question must be faced: How much heterogeneity can these nations tolerate without changing their entire identity? When does a Turk become German? When does a Filipino become Japanese? When does a Mexican become American? The last example is plausible in that countries like the United States have been built on immigration—they are, by nature, somewhat heterogeneous, although there is some question as to how much more diversity can be tolerated. For the other two examples—Turks and Filipinos—the answer is far more complex given the relative homogeneity of the receiving countries. This is a major reason why we have argued that these changing demographic patterns could become the biggest challenge of the early 21st century.

Increased Fertility

There is a way out of this demographic quandary: increased fertility among the resident population. In countries such as Germany and Japan, fertility is at an all-time low. A very slight change in fertility can yield noteworthy results a few years later. With slightly higher but still below-replacement-level fertility (e.g., 1.8), immigration levels could be substantially reduced. Heilig and his colleagues prepared a "demographic revival" projection for Germany where fertility rises to 2.1 and immigration increases to 300,000 persons per year. The end result is a German population of 95 million and still growing by 2050. But such levels of fertility and immigration are not necessary for Germany to maintain approximately its current population size.

We have prepared a projection for Germany assuming that fertility would rise to 1.8 and that immigration would be limited to 80,000 annually. If one favors population limitation and reduced immigration, the results are quite encouraging. Germany's population would rise from 83 million in 2000 to 86 million in 2015 before beginning a very slow decline. By 2050, it would total 77 million. Its "active age" population (15–64) would drop from 55 million to 50 million in 2030 and to 45 million by 2050. A similar demographic pattern could also apply to countries such as France, Great Britain, Japan, and others where fertility currently is extremely low.

All of this invites the question, How can fertility be raised slightly? France, for example, has tried for decades to encourage families to have more children, without any success. "In Japan, a rising generation of educated women resent the traditional expectation that they become full-time housewives after college, bringing up children in cramped accommodations while their husbands are absent from early morning to late evening."[50] One German state (Brandenburg) offers a payment of $650 for every child born. "Eastern Germany's adults appear to have come as close to a temporary suspension of childbearing as any large population in the human experience."[51] Similar attitudes no doubt exist in Italy, Spain, and the United Kingdom.

However, there is compelling evidence that slightly higher fertility could be attained under certain circumstances. In recent years, Sweden and other Scandinavian countries have provided excellent examples. In Sweden, fertility rose from 1.6 in 1986 (when it was among the lowest in the world) to 2.0 in 1990. It remains at that level today. Norway's fertility rate is 1.9; Finland's, 1.8. Research suggests that "the reason could be a mixture of excellent social provisions (paid maternity and paternity leave, child care, kindergarten, comfortable housing) together with a significant degree of overall gender equality, measured, for example, in the numbers of female politicians and cabinet ministers."[52] European nations and Japan would do well to examine the Swedish system. It might provide an answer to their demographic dilemma.

The population dilemma will eventually play itself out. Some increased diversity will occur in the industrialized nations. The question remains, How much diversity and what will it mean to the sociocultural nature of these societies? If population limits are desired, immigration levels must be reduced. The question is, How and by how much? Whatever the answer, it won't be easy to implement. If the immigration problem is ever to be alleviated, fertility in developing countries must fall rapidly, and this must begin immediately. Yet the U.S. Congress has repeatedly cut the budget for international family planning assistance. Fortunately, the 1997 and 1998 sessions, with pressure from the Clinton administration, raised the allocation once again, though slightly.

The momentum for growth is enormous, reflecting the high fertility of recent decades. Moderate declines in fertility, as have been reported recently in the media, will not suffice. Countries such as Costa Rica, Sri Lanka, Mexico, and Bangladesh, among others, have already exhibited moderate declines; however, the three-child family will continue to fuel population growth when so many young couples are available to have those children. Reducing fertility in the short term will help to diffuse the pressure for emigration.

The 1996 UN medium projections have been used in this study. How reliable are they? Of course, we never know what will happen in the future. However, the UN's medium scenario seems quite reasonable, although it is difficult to imagine a 2050 world total fertility rate of 2.1 or Nigeria with a rate of 2.5. If anything, the projections are on the low side. Yet even before their official publication in 1998, advocates (as well as the mass media) jumped on the bandwagon and proclaimed an end to population growth on planet Earth!

A few examples are in order. A UPI story commented: "[T]he planet-threatening human population boom is at an end. It suggests that overpopulation, leading to food shortages, ozone holes, unemployment, acid rain, war, environmental poisoning, ominous climatic changes, and other catastrophic assaults on Mother Earth, is in abeyance."[53] A *Wall Street Journal* article stated that much of the world will soon be in a "demographic free fall" and used the occasion to castigate the "population control crowd." A *New York Times* article carried the following headline: "How to Fix a Crowded World: Add More People." The ubiquitous Ben Wattenberg reappeared in another *New York Times* magazine article, titled "The Population Explosion Is Over." Interestingly, most of these reports concentrated on the low scenario of the UN projections, where all nations' fertility eventually falls (or rises) to 2.1 or lower—obviously a strictly demographic exercise that does not represent reality. Perhaps these authors (certainly not demographers) should have paid more attention to the statement by demographer Joseph Chamie, chief author of the report: "[U]nless couples have access to safe contraceptives compatible with their cultural and religious beliefs, they are limited in how they can fulfill their hopes of smaller families, and population declines are much slower."[54]

In this chapter we have reviewed the regional scenarios, the age scenario, and industrial countries with and without immigration. An additional factor that will influence future demographic trends is AIDS. In chapter 9 we categorize the countries of the world by both current fertility rates and the intensity of the AIDS epidemic as we consider the prescription for the 21st century.

CHAPTER 4

Immigration

If demography is destiny, population movements are the motor of history. In centuries past, differential growth rates, economic conditions, and governmental policies have produced massive migrations by Greeks, Jews, Germanic tribes, Norse, Turks, Russians, Chinese, and others.[55]

This fact has not changed and perhaps will not change in the foreseeable future. As the planet's population continues to increase by 100 million persons each year, with growth rates being significantly higher in the developing countries, the importance of migration both internal and international is being emphasized. Scholars and policymakers alike are becoming aware of migration's tremendous effect on urban growth and international relations.

Homo sapiens has never been a sedentary animal. On the contrary, humans have always been extremely peripatetic. Perhaps it is necessary for humankind to move on if it is to progress. The English philosopher Alfred North Whitehead once wrote: "Animals that wander must adapt or die. When man ceases to wander, he will cease to ascend in the scale of being."[56] International movements of people are as old as history and even prehistory, but little information exists on the size and nature of such movements before the 19th century.

Exploration had a great role in making possible the early migrations. In the 15th and 16th centuries, men like Marco Polo, Columbus, and Magellan set out to satisfy the curiosity of governments eager to know what riches lay over the horizon. Settlement often followed in later centuries. The Portuguese started colonies in Africa; the Spaniards, English, Dutch, and French in the Americas; and the English in Australia and New Zealand. But as we look at the racial composition of certain countries today, we can only conclude that other types of perhaps smaller migratory movements also took place centuries ago (e.g., the Japanese in South America, the Caucasian "redlegs" in Barbados and other West Indies islands, the Ainu in Japan). One can drive along a dusty road in Cameroon and observe a Lebanese Maronite church. Whitehead need not have worried. Humankind is and always has been extremely mobile.[57]

With population increasing throughout the world and with faster means of transportation and improved communication, international migration has increased in recent centuries. More people are international migrants today than at any previous time in history. Since the end of World War II, the pressures to migrate have intensified, a trend expected to continue; however, these pressures do not necessarily result in actual international migration. That depends on many other factors. Exactly what are the pressures that increase the potential for international migration?[58]

First, the dramatic *increases in population* in typical sending countries have led to rapid labor-force growth, as we have seen. The growth has been especially large among young-adult age groups, who are known to have the highest migration propensities. Such growth will continue. Over the 1990–2010 period, labor-force growth in the developing world is projected to be even larger than it was in the 1970–1990 period—733 million compared to 658 million.

Second, *economic differentials* between most industrialized nations and most developing regions are bound to increase. Other factors being equal, increasing differentials in real wages and standards of living should be expected to increase the incentives favoring international migration.

Third, *technological advances*, especially in transportation and communication, have affected previously isolated populations in developing regions. Millions of people now can access the means to move internationally. Long-distance intercontinental moves have become quick and inexpensive. Film and television, especially Cable News

Network (CNN), have brought to the attention of remote millions the economic attractions of life in other areas. International telephone and fax communications have allowed migrants to maintain close ties with family and friends. Together, these technological advances are contributing to increased immigration.

Fourth, with growing levels of immigration come *increases in social networks* across international borders. "The existence of family and community networks . . . in more affluent countries make the migration decision easier."[59] Generally, family reunification follows the initial outflow of workers. With increased family movements, social networks between the places of origin and destination evolve what might be called the "anchor impact." "The potential for future immigration depends primarily on the magnitude of previous immigration and the size and geographic distribution of family networks of previous immigrants."[60]

Fifth, some governments actively promote the *export of labor* as a matter of economic policy. Examples include Turkey, the Philippines, India, Jamaica, and Mexico.

Finally, an *increase in violence, repression, persecution, and ethnic tensions*, particularly in countries that already have large and diverse populations, is a major contributor to international migration.

Together these factors almost guarantee an increase in the *desire* to emigrate in future years. Whether that desire is followed by actual migration remains to be seen and is dependent on numerous other factors such as the willingness of the potential receiving countries to accept these migrants. In the 1940s much international migration was of a distressed or forced character rather than representing the usual peacetime response to economic opportunity.

Not all post–World War II movements were so traumatic. As the world gradually settled down to a more peaceful existence, Europe again assumed a major place in the overall migration picture. Indeed, the exodus from Europe in the 25 years from 1956 to 1980 reached at least 8 million, with Australia, Canada, and the United States the principal target countries. "In 1990 legal international migrants numbered about 100 million, refugees about 19 million, and illegal migrants probably at least 10 million."[61] The increased flow to Australia and South Africa in this period reflects those countries' special efforts to encourage European immigration. The decrease in the number of Europeans moving to Latin America is attributed to the attraction of high wages and good job opportunities for southern European workers in countries closer to home, coinciding with Latin American measures to slow the intake of unskilled migrant workers. The drop in migration to Canada and the United States is associated in part with the favorable work situation in western Europe and some decline in industrial activity in North America.

Europe, especially the north and west, has itself been a target for intercontinental immigrants. People from Algeria, Tunisia, Morocco, Turkey, and the Netherlands Antilles and Surinam have flocked to the Netherlands, France, West Germany, and Switzerland—many as temporary workers. The mid-1950s saw the start of an important migration into the United Kingdom from the newly independent countries of the British Commonwealth, mainly the West Indies, India, and Pakistan. The 1971 British census showed that a total of 680,000 persons born in the new Commonwealth nations had entered the United Kingdom since 1961. In 1992, however, Britain reduced the number of people granted asylum from more than 20,000 to less than 10,000. "Overall in the mid-1990s western European countries were moving inexorably toward reducing to a minimum—if not totally eliminating—immigration from non-European countries."[62]

The United Nations estimated that in 1972, 7.3 million migrants were legally working in western Europe; with their dependents, this meant a known foreign population of nearly 12 million. Adding in clandestine immigrants may have put the total as high as 13 million. Many of these 13 million came not from other continents but from lesser developed European neighbors. France, for example, counted over 4 million foreign-born residents in 1976—about 8 percent of the country's population. Many of these came from Spain, Portugal, and Italy. By the mid-1970s, migratory movements slowed in Europe as a result of restrictive measures taken in both sending and receiving countries, as well as other factors, including rising unemployment among native workers.

It should not be assumed that intra-European migration is a new phenomenon. It was extensive more than a century ago. In 1880, there were already 1 million foreigners in France. In the decades before

World War I and between the world wars, foreign workers streamed into Germany, mostly from eastern and southern European countries. In 1910, foreigners represented 3.5 percent of the population of Belgium and 15 percent of that of Switzerland—a proportion not much lower than today's 20 percent. This recent—and as we shall see, continuing—movement across European national borders is but a resumption and an increase in the ongoing process of people moving about in search of a better way of life.

Recent international migration has not been focused solely on Europe. About 300,000 Japanese were in Brazil by the close of World War II. That number now approaches 750,000. Between 1946 and 1957, Argentina accepted over 600,000 immigrants, Brazil some 450,000, and Venezuela about 400,000. Many of these came from Italy, Spain, Germany, and Portugal. Some intracontinental migration has also occurred. Movements between El Salvador and Honduras followed the Soccer War in 1969, and flows continue between Colombia and Venezuela and from Bolivia, Paraguay, and Chile to Argentina and Brazil.

Since the end of World War II, the balance of migration has increasingly shifted toward North America and, to some extent, Oceania. These two were the only major world regions to record net in-migration during the 1950s. Out-migration from Europe decreased substantially from a net loss of 5.4 million in the 1947–1956 period to 0.3 million during the 1960s, while speeding up in Asia. Both Latin America and Africa switched from positive to negative net migration between these two 10-year periods. Insofar as only migration is concerned, this trend appears to continue today.

The United States has always been a destination country. Indeed, migration to the United States had already been occurring for several centuries before its independence in 1776. Colonial immigrants came primarily from Great Britain and northwestern Europe and settled in areas already inhabited by Native Americans. Thus, the land area now occupied by the 48 contiguous states has repeatedly seen the settlement of one group followed by the immigration of another. Between the end of the Revolutionary War and 1819, when immigrants were first counted officially, an estimated 250,000 foreign-born persons had arrived by ship. Between 1820 and 1995, the recorded number of immigrants added up to 62 million. The peak intercensual decade was 1901–1910, with 8.8 million recorded immigrants, while the peak decade until very recently was 1905–1914, with a count of 10.1 million. The record single year was 1907, when 1,285,349 immigrants were counted. That figure was approached again in 1914. Until recently, recorded annual immigration has been averaging about half that number. However, adding in plausible estimates of illegal immigration, which range up to 500,000 a year, brings current immigration levels up to and higher than any previous highs—perhaps well over 1 million annually.

The extent of immigration, especially in the early 20th century, led to the passage of restrictive legislation limiting such movements, culminating in the Quota Acts of the 1920s. Legal immigration numbers have risen steadily since the acts' 1965 amendments took effect in 1968. The Immigration and Naturalization Service (INS) figures on legally admitted immigrants are 373,000 for 1970, 531,000 for 1980, and 1.5 million for 1990. More dramatic has been the change in the origins of legal immigrants. The proportion of immigrants from the traditional sending countries of Europe shrank to just 11 percent in 1981–1985, while the share of Asian immigrants soared to 48 percent. The size of the flow from Latin America rose, but its share of the total fell from 40 percent in 1971–1980 to 35 percent in 1981–1985. This pattern continues.

The recent increase in immigrants has reversed a 60-year decline in the proportion of foreign-born U.S. residents. That proportion fell from 14.7 percent in 1910 to 4.7 percent in 1970, but it had risen to 6.2 percent by 1980 and to about 10 percent by 1995. While the 62 million immigrants since 1820 have come from all parts of the globe, different countries or regions of origin have dominated the flow at different times. Most important has been the ongoing shift in the composition of the immigrant population from European to Latin American and Asian. Immigrants from northern and western Europe dominated through most of the 19th century, and it was not until the 20th century that they made up less than half of total immigration. By 1980–1985, 48 percent of all immigrants to the United States came from Asia and 35 percent came from Latin America and the Caribbean. This is a major shift from less than a century ago

(1901–1920), when 41 percent came from northern and western Europe, 44 percent came from southern and eastern Europe, a mere 4 percent came from Latin America, and another 4 percent came from Asia. This shift in country or region of origin is destined to continue in future years.

With the growing extent of international migration throughout the world, most countries (165 in the United Nations) began to require passports and visas so as to regulate the number of people crossing international borders.[63] According to data from the United Nations, during this past decade, Europe, North America, and Oceania had net population gains from international migration. On the other hand, Africa, Asia, and Latin America had net losses.[64] Looking at table 4.1, derived from the UN report, we can see that international migration also occurred within regions. Africa, for example, had net out-migration over the first five years of the 1990s. But this was not true of southern, northern, and central Africa. Similarly, Europe gained in net migration, but this was concentrated in the western European countries.

How does immigration (or emigration, for that matter) affect the countries involved? To a considerable extent, it depends on the population size of the country itself. For example, the United States received more than four times the number of immigrants than Canada in the mid-1990s, yet the rate of net migration is higher in Canada because its population is only one-tenth the size of the U.S. population.[65] It is important to bear in mind that the impact of migration also is related to the natural increase (i.e., births minus deaths) in that country. For example, if in some future year more deaths than births took place in the United States, then over 100 percent of any population increase would be accounted for by immigration. This is already the case in Germany, as it is in some Florida counties.

More people are international migrants today than at any previous time in history. Indeed,

> the magnitudes of human flows across national boundaries have become very large over the past three decades . . . as of the late 1980s some 80 million persons were resident outside their nations of citizenship; conservatively, these numbers are likely to have reached 100

million since the dissolution of the former Soviet Union and are expected to increase further in the coming decades.[66]

Compared to changing fertility and mortality, adjusting migration seems fairly simple. Mandating certain levels of fertility is not only highly unethical, it is almost impossible to enforce, and of course limiting life expectancy for demographic reasons is inhumane. It should be the goal of humankind to extend healthy lives as long as possible and to compensate for such success by reductions in fertility and/or

REGION	NET MIGRANTS (000S)	RATE (PER 1,000 POP.)
SENDING REGIONS		
Africa	-63	-0.1
Eastern	-128	-0.6
Central	4	0.1
Northern	69	0.5
Southern	2	0.04
Western	-10	-0.1
Asia	-1,366	-0.4
Eastern	-171	-0.1
South Central	-664	-0.5
Southeastern	-485	-1.1
Western	-46	-0.3
Latin America	-392	-0.9
Caribbean	-99	-2.9
Central America	-202	-1.7
South America	-91	-0.3
RECEIVING REGIONS		
Europe	739	1
Eastern	-109	-0.4
Northern	47	0.5
Southern	-20	-0.1
Western	821	4.6
North America	971	3.4
Oceania	111	4
Australia–New Zealand	122	5.8
Other Oceania	-11	-1.7

Table 4.1—Migrant Sending and Receiving Regions, 1990–1995

Source: United Nations, *World Population Prospects, The 1994 Revision* (New York: United Nations, 1995), 128.

immigration. International migration can be predetermined, at least in theory. The world is comprised of some 165 independent states, and all can place limits on in- or out-migration, if they so desire. Most of them do, but does it work? The evidence of recent decades suggests that arbitrary limitations on immigration do not work very well. As long as the number of young adults in the typical sending countries continues to grow, the prospects are dim that such strict limitations can be successful.

For answers to the question of how to reduce immigration, we must turn to the traditional approaches—"push" and "pull." Receiving countries must make themselves less attractive to newcomers, thereby reducing the "pull" factor; sending countries must become more attractive to their own people, thus reducing the "push" factor. The industrialized countries could tighten their immigration laws and better enforce their restrictions. Legal immigration could be limited to those people who can contribute directly to the betterment of the host society. Language requirements could be more strongly enforced. As to clandestine movements, which are growing,[67] more rigid border patrols as well as tamperproof identity cards would aid considerably in reducing the extent of such movements. The typical receiving countries can limit and reduce immigration, legal and illegal, if they are willing to put such restrictions into effect.[68] Then, potential immigrants would not be as likely to be "pulled" to such countries.

A more humane approach to limiting immigration would be to de-emphasize the "push" factors through economic and social development in developing regions. This can be done only through massive economic assistance from the richer to the poorer countries. Basically, people would prefer not to move to strange and sometimes hostile foreign lands; they are forced to do so to better their "lot in life." If their lot in life could be improved at home, immigration could be reduced substantially.

Development for its own sake should be encouraged wherever it is feasible. However, development to curtail immigration is seldom successful in the short run. Indeed, development increases rather than reduces the impetus for migration, as people begin to realize that conditions are far better in the industrialized regions than they are in their own "developing" areas. With the completion of economic modernization and with lower fertility, however, the pool of potential migrants in future generations could diminish. Perhaps the best example of such a situation is the South Korean economic phenomenon. Countries such as Mexico, Indonesia, and Brazil may follow in Korea's footsteps.

Population and immigration problems are already here, and we must be concerned with the short term. The industrialized countries must therefore make every effort to establish reasonable and humane limits on immigration and, at the same time, assist the developing countries both economically and demographically. As we look at the recent massive movements of refugees and other migrants across international borders, it is clear that thus far trying to limit immigration is not working. What are the alternatives? If we rely on Weberian "ideal types," two extreme models can be visualized: all borders are closed completely, or immigration is open totally throughout the world.

Some people in industrialized countries argue for an end to immigration, usually for their own nation, without any comment on what other advanced countries should do. "Germany for Germans," "Japan for the Japanese" are the cries heard from some groups. Under such policies, the pent-up potential for migration would be exacerbated a thousandfold. One can hardly imagine such a world and can only speculate on the violence that such policies would create. Other people in both industrialized and developing regions argue for open borders. In the United States, the *Wall Street Journal* editorializes annually for the need to open the nation's borders to all. Such a scenario would lead to disaster—environmentally, economically, and demographically. We can only speculate on the interracial violence that would ensue.

Rather than opt for these extremes, the nations of the world should begin to think more globally in the early part of the 21st century. For example, problems in Nigeria should be of concern to people in Switzerland. The world is shrinking rapidly through communications and transportation advances. Both the industrial and the developing countries must adjust to an entirely new and challenging demographic situation. The richer countries, while maintaining low fertility, should continue to accept limited numbers of immigrants under certain conditions. More important, these nations should accept the fact that in the process, their identity will change, albeit very gradually. It is relatively easy for Americans and Canadians to accept limited numbers of newcomers. Their countries are continually redefining themselves and are truly nations of immigrants. Such is not the case in Germany and Japan, however. These countries might follow the examples set by Americans and Canadians—accept limited numbers of newcomers and assimilate them into their cultures. The question Can a Turk ever become a German? should no longer be asked, especially of the second generation. To survive as independent nations in the 21st century, receiving countries will have to adjust culturally and ethnically to an entirely new situation. It will not be easy, but it must take place.[69]

One major problem in some European countries will concern the Arab population. Do Europeans want Arabs to assimilate? Equally important, do the Arabs desire to *be* assimilated? "European societies generally either do not want to assimilate immigrants or have great difficulty doing so, and the degree to which Muslim immigrants and their children want to be assimilated is unclear. Hence sustained substantial immigration is likely to produce countries divided into Christian and Muslim communities."[70]

If the immigration problem is ever to be alleviated, population growth in developing countries must fall. Without declines in fertility, there can be little hope for reductions in immigration. But this is not a hopeless situation. "There is a strong grassroots demand, much of it still unmet: an estimated 100 million additional women worldwide report that they would like to use contraceptives if they had access to the necessary information and supplies."[71] The momentum for growth is enormous, reflecting the high fertility of recent decades. Thus, moderate declines in fertility will not suffice—countries such as Costa Rica, Sri Lanka, and Mexico have already exhibited moderate declines. Reducing fertility is one means of assuring that eventually immigration will no longer pose a major problem for all. Without such demographic shifts, the threats made by the late prime minister Houari Boumedienne of Algeria will be proven true: "No quantity of atomic bombs could stem the tide of billions . . . who will some day leave the poor southern part of the world to erupt into the relatively accessible spaces of the rich northern hemisphere looking for survival."[72] Such thinking remains prevalent today. On 5 May 1997, Mahathir Bin

Mohamad, the prime minister of Malaysia, had these words to say to a South African group:

> The north can gain much by recolonizing. But we do have the ultimate weapon. People are more mobile now. They can go anywhere. In a borderless world we can go anywhere. If we are not allowed a good life in our countries, if we are going to be global citizens, then we should migrate north. We should migrate north in our millions, legally or illegally. Masses of Asians and Africans should inundate Europe and America. If there is any strength that we have, it is in the numbers. Three-fourths of the world is either black, brown, yellow, or some combination of all these. We will make all nations in the world rainbow nations.[73]

The 21st century will indeed be a period of demographic crisis, be it fertility or immigration. However, such a crisis does not have to occur if population growth is reduced and if some of the low-fertility nations accept limited numbers of immigrants and assimilate them into their societies.

Conclusion

The late, great American demographer Kingsley Davis once stated: "Although particular migration streams are temporary, migration pressure is perpetual because it is inherent in technological inequality."[74] Today, international migration reflects the inequality between less developed, developing, and developed nations or, in sociologist Anthony Richmond's terms, gemeinschaft (traditional), gesellschaft (industrial), and verbindungsnetschaft (postindustrial).[75] A majority of migrants are coming to postindustrial countries such as the United States from less industrial or traditional countries of origin. In Europe, people leave the more traditional areas of southeastern countries and move to gesellschaft western Europe. At the same time, patterns of natural growth are changing. In most countries of origin, fertility remains high while mortality is rapidly declining. The resulting growth is exerting tremendous pressure on these societies. One obvious solution is emigration to technologically advanced regions.

Another new situation exists at the receiving end. Countries of western Europe as well as Canada, Australia, and the United States are all experiencing extremely low fertility. A number of European countries—both western and eastern—as well as Japan, now have natural decreases, that is, fewer births than deaths. Others are barely increasing. In the long run, most presently developed countries will just replace their populations or actually decrease in numbers if current trends continue. International migration will be the only way to maintain population growth, if that is considered desirable.

The effects of international migration are awesome when the other demographic variables are changing in such a way that on the one hand, some developing countries can survive only through emigration, yet on the other hand, all future growth in some developed countries can come only from immigration. The complexions of entire societies may be altered—the results of such migration patterns interacting with changing fertility and mortality. Two recent examples are Belize, in Central America, and Kosovo, in southeast Europe.

Kingsley Davis has concluded that international migration will continue as long as there is technological inequality. Paul Kennedy has commented on the same situation. As long as humans have been on this planet, there have been migrants in search of a better life. This was true of early nomads, of rampaging hordes, of colonists, and of individual migrants, legal or illegal. It will be true tomorrow as well. Said Davis, writing in 1939: "The nationalistic control of migration has led to a peculiar world situation. Demographically, the potential migration pent up in today's world is enormous. . . . One wonders how long the inequalities of growth between major regions can continue without an explosion that will somehow quickly restore the balance."[76] These words remain relevant for the 21st century.

Ironically, many years after Davis wrote those prophetic words, then President Boumedienne of Algeria reminded us all in the similar, though much more dismal, words that were cited above. As recently as 1996, economist Lester Thurow referred to the future problem of demography "with the rich world's aging population facing a tide of immigration from the poor world."[77]

The extent of future migration is inexorably tied to population growth and environmental quality. Partly through migration, the population has spread around the planet. No longer are unoccupied "safety valves" available. Yet if population pressures persist in some parts of the globe and if resources become scarcer, is it not reasonable to expect that *Homo sapiens* will continue to migrate in even larger numbers in search of food, shelter, and a better way of life? Throughout history, this has been humankind's way of solving resource problems. Why not in 2000 or 2010? Perhaps Boumedienne (as well as Davis and Thurow) will prove to be an accurate prophet.

At present, free international migration is no longer feasible on the societal level. But on the individual level, it remains a possible solution to intolerable living conditions. There is a clear conflict between the interests of the individual and those of the society. Free and unfettered migration for all of humankind might be a possibility. However, as John Tanton reminded us years ago,

> Happily, it is possible to envision a world in which international migration could become free and unfettered. Appropriately, it is the world of the stationary state, in which people in different regions are in equilibrium with resources and in which there is a reasonable chance in each region for self-fulfillment, matched with social equity. Under these conditions, international migration could be unfettered, because there would be little incentive to move.[78]

International migration is intertwined with continued population growth. The combination of both processes has resulted in today's and tomorrow's enormous urban entities. Much of what was beautiful has disappeared from the planet—the result of these two forces simultaneously at work. It may be time to reflect on the wisdom of John Stuart Mill, who wrote in 1857,

> If the earth must lose that great portion of its pleasantness which it owes to things that the unlimited increase of wealth and population would extirpate from it, for the mere purpose of enabling it to support a larger, but not a happier or a better population, I sincerely hope, for the sake of posterity, that they will be content to be stationary, long before necessity compels them to it.[79]

CHAPTER 5

The Three Demographic Billionaires: China, India, and the Muslim World

Introduction

In the previous chapters, little, if anything, was mentioned about China and India. These two giant nations, both with over 1 billion people each, have such huge populations that any demographic changes in either, or both, would strongly affect the growth rates for their regions. Thus, although they have been included in earlier projections as appropriate, a brief discussion of each—and both together—is warranted. Also to be considered is the Muslim world, composed of over 1 billion people spread out among numerous countries.

China has had at least 1 billion inhabitants since about 1985; India will join this very elite group in the year 2000, according to the medium projections of the United Nations. Thus, at the start of the 21st century, China and India combined will have a total of about 2.3 billion inhabitants. To put it another way, at the turn of the century, China's and India's populations together will represent about 40 percent of the world's people! Since China, especially, also has a very large overseas population, the Chinese diaspora may add a few more hundreds of millions to that total. India's overseas population, while not as large as China's, also contributes to the amazing size of those two groups of people. If overseas Chinese and Indians are included in the totals , they may comprise close to half the world's population today. But let us concentrate solely on the countries themselves.

China

As recently as 1950, China's population was about 550 million, and it had a total fertility rate of 6.2. One can only speculate on its size today if it had followed the pattern of other developing nations by maintaining a high fertility rate. Instead, the Chinese government—realizing that such growth could never be maintained—introduced a very strict fertility limitation program. It was interrupted during the "Cultural Revolution" in the late 1960s and early 1970s, and the fertility rate rose from 5.6 to 6.1. However, since 1970 that rate has fallen rapidly as the government instituted what are considered by some to be draconian measures of population control. "Stop at Two" became a strong motto, and even the one-child family was advocated. By 1990, the total fertility rate had fallen below replacement (1.92) and has continued to fall to about 1.8 at the present time. Over the same 1950–2000 period, life expectancy at birth has risen from 40.8 to 71 years. Thus, while fertility has fallen rapidly, mortality too has exhibited major declines. The result of this demographic revolution has led to an estimated population in the year 2000 of 1,220,224,000 (1.2 billion).

What about the future? With fertility below replacement, will China's population begin to fall? According to the UN medium projections, the population will continue to grow until 2040, when it will reach about 1.6 billion. It will then begin a slow decrease to 1.5 billion in 2050, at which time its rate of growth will be –.01. However, this scenario assumes that fertility will once again climb slightly in the next century, reaching 2.1 in 2020–2025, and remain at that level thereafter. With all the pressure from the government to limit families to one child or two at the most, it is difficult to accept the assumption that fertility will rise in the next century. Perhaps the "low scenario" is more appropriate for China and more closely represents the government's desires. According to this scenario, fertility would continue falling to 1.5 by 2005–2010 and remain at that level to 2050. If this were to occur, the population would still grow for a while, peaking in 2025 at just under 1.4 billion and falling thereafter to under 1.2 billion in 2050, when its growth rate would be –0.76. China's population in 2050 would be slightly smaller than it is today and would be falling very gradually.

Can this low scenario be achieved? Yes, if the government continues to advocate strongly the one-child family and if other nations— mainly the United States—stop meddling in what is an obvious internal matter. Far too often, conservative U.S. congressmembers have interfered in these Chinese internal affairs by blocking any assistance if abortion was encouraged in China. This is an internal ethical decision that must be decided by the Chinese alone. If we are concerned about population growth on this planet, we should laud the Chinese efforts rather than demean them. Consider what that country's population would be without such "draconian" fertility measures.

Given the expected demographic behavior of the Chinese in the first half of the 21st century, significant changes in age composition can be assumed. Often, these shifts prove to be as troublesome as sheer population growth. Consider that, following the medium UN scenario, China's share of elderly (65 and over) will rise from 6.7 percent in 2000 to 19.2 percent in 2050, which translates into 300 million "elderly"— more than today's total U.S. population. On the other hand, and due to very low fertility, the share under age 25 will drop quite rapidly. Taking care of 300 million elderly is a challenge of enormous proportions.

Another matter to consider when looking at China is its phenomenal economic growth in recent years. The standard of living is rising rapidly, and a few "capitalistic" ideas are being accepted. All of this is resulting in a richer diet and demands for more goods and services. With such an enormous population size, it has been estimated that with continued economic progress, China's needs for wheat early in the next century will surpass the amount used by the rest of the world today! Similar projections can be made for other resources. While China's economic progress is a great temptation for American and other business enterprises, it also is a major and possibly tragic development as it affects resources and the environment.

Whatever scenario is followed in the 21st century, China will play a major role on the world stage. As Samuel Huntington has stated:

> It appears probable that for most of history, China had the world's largest economy. The diffusion of technology and the economic development of non-Western societies in the second half of the 20th century are now producing a return to the historical pattern. This will be a slow process, but by the middle of the 21st century, if not before, the distribution of economic product and manufacturing output among the leading civilizations is likely to resemble that of 1800. The 200-year Western "blip" on the world economy will be over.[80]

India

Let us turn now to the second demographic soon-to-be-billionaire. India is an excellent example of a country that has had some success in lowering its fertility in recent years—but still more needs to be done.

In 1950, India's population stood at 358 million, Indian women averaged 6 births, and life expectancy was 38.7 years at birth. By 1995, fertility had been cut in half. Women averaged just over 3 births and life expectancy was up to 60.5 years—a tremendous demographic achievement in only 45 years. However, during that same period (1950–1995) India's population rose to 929 million. This increase can be attributed to continued relatively high fertility over the period as well as increased life expectancy.

What about the future? Once again, we turn to the latest UN medium projections and note that India's population will continue growing to 1 billion at the millennium (2000) and reach 1.5 billion by 2050. By that year it will have surpassed China and be the nation with the largest population in the world. This projection is based on the assumption that India's total fertility rate will continue to fall, reaching 2.1 in 2010–2015 and remaining at that level thereafter. Life expectancy is also expected to increase to 75 years in 2050. At that time, India's rate of growth will be a minuscule 0.42. Given that the fertility is already down to just over 3 births per woman, such a projection appears quite reasonable, bearing in mind that it is more difficult for fertility to fall from 3 to 2 than from, say, 6 to 5. India must continue emphasizing the small-family norm and improve family planning services. If that is done, the goal of zero population growth can be reached shortly after 2050.

India also will be faced with rapid changes in age composition in the 21st century. The elderly population is expected to increase from 5 percent in 2000 to 15.2 percent in 2050. That translates into about 233 million individuals compared to fewer than 50 million today. The challenge for the nation will be formidable. On the other hand, the share under age 25 will fall, especially as fertility continues to drop. This may allow for better education of children, but one wonders if care for the elderly will be so expensive that educational improvements will be impossible to attain.

As with China, India is also experiencing rapid economic growth, although not on the scale displayed by its larger neighbor. Nevertheless, the entire world must be made aware that soon India will be placing more demands—for richer food and more consumer products—on a world already uncertain about its resource limitations.

Combining the Two Giants

Earlier we pointed out that, added together, over 40 percent of the world's population resides in these two countries. Again we ask, What about the future? By 2050, according to the UN's medium projection, their combined population will be just over 3 billion in a world of 9.3 billion inhabitants. Thus, their share will have fallen to about one-third of the world's total. This, of course, reflects the already low birth rates—especially in China—and the projection that these rates will fall further in India. Nevertheless, to a considerable extent the demographic fate of planet Earth depends on what happens in these two giant countries. Any shift in attitude toward higher fertility would prove disastrous not only for China and India but for the entire world.

The Muslim World

It is difficult, if not impossible, to compare the Muslim world with China and India. One reason is that no single country predominates in the Muslim world. However, since the population in almost all

Muslim-dominated countries is expected to rise rapidly in the foreseeable future, and since the Muslim faith is gaining strength almost everywhere, a look at its demographic growth is appropriate at this time. It is also important to point out that we are now witnessing what political scientist Samuel Huntington has called an "Islamic Resurgence": "Beginning in 1970, Islamic symbols, beliefs, institutions, policies, and organizations won increasing commitment and support throughout the world of one billion Muslims, stretching from Morocco to Indonesia and from Nigeria to Kazakhstan."[81] Here we must warn the reader that taking a count of religious bodies is a very uncertain task. However, our data are fairly reliable and are mostly derived from Samuel Huntington's *The Clash of Civilizations.*

World population has grown at a rate of about 1.8 percent per year over the past 30 years; however, in predominantly Muslim countries, growth rates have been almost always well over 2 percent. Indeed, they reached 3 percent in certain years.

> Between 1965 and 1990, . . . the Maghreb population increased at a rate of 2.65 percent a year, from 29.8 million to 59 million, with Algerians multiplying at a 3 percent annual rate. During these same years, the number of Egyptians rose at a 2.3 percent rate from 29.4 million to 52.4 million. In central Asia, between 1970 and 1993, populations grew at rates of 2.9 percent in Tajikstan, 2.6 percent in Uzbekistan, 2.5 percent in Turkmenistan, 1.9 percent in Kyrgyzstan, but only 1.1 percent in Kazakhstan, whose population is almost half Russian. Pakistan and Bangladesh had population growth rates exceeding 2.5 percent a year, while Indonesia's was over 2.0 percent a year. Overall, Muslims . . . constituted perhaps 18 percent of the world's population in 1980 [or about 800 million] and are likely to be over 20 percent in 2000 [or about 1.2 billion] and 30 percent in 2025 [or about 2.4 billion].[82]

Recall that the world population in 2025 will approximate 8 billion. Should the percentage of Muslims continue to increase even slightly to, say, 35 percent by 2025, the Muslim population in the world would total about 3.3 billion people.

Given that the Muslim population is demographically "young," continued growth can be expected for some time unless fertility rates fall dramatically. Furthermore, increases (or attempted increases) in international migration are sure to follow. It is not inappropriate, then, to quote Huntington's insightful statement:

> Larger populations need more resources, and hence people from societies with dense and/or rapidly growing populations tend to push outward, occupy territory, and exert pressure on other less demographically dynamic peoples. Islamic population growth is thus a major contributing factor to the conflicts along the borders of the Islamic world between Muslims and other peoples. Population pressure combined with economic stagnation promotes Muslim migration to Western and other non-Muslim societies, elevating immigration as an issue in those societies. The juxtaposition of a rapidly growing people of one culture and a slowly growing or stagnant people of another culture generates pressures for economic and/or political adjustment in both societies. In the 1970s, for instance, the demographic balance in the former Soviet Union shifted drastically with Muslims increasing by 24 percent while Russians increased by 6.5 percent, causing great concern among Central Asian communist leaders. Similarly, rapid growth in the number of Albanians does not reassure Serbs, Greeks, or Italians. Israelis are concerned about the high growth rates of Palestinians, and Spain with a population growing at less than one-fifth of 1 percent a year, is uneasy confronted by Maghreb neighbors with population growing more than ten times as fast and per capita GNP's about one-tenth of their own.[83]

The major argument in part I of this book is that fertility levels—while diminishing—need to continue their downward trend for the sake of improving living conditions in developing countries and ensuring stability at the international level. Immigration, the "safety valve" of the past, no longer constitutes a "solution" to population growth. In part II, we review the progress made to date in slowing population growth at the global level through family planning and improved economic conditions. We consider the politics encompassing the international population movement, and we outline a prescription for the 21st century, taking into account an unwelcome addition to the demographic equation in the past 20 years: the AIDS epidemic.

Response to Rapid Population Growth

CHAPTER 6

Support for International Population Assistance

Emergence of Concern over Demographic Trends

Concern over rapid population growth began in the aftermath of World War II, as a small group of academics and private-foundation leaders began to realize the potential consequences of exponential population growth for the planet. This group developed a policy-oriented demographic discipline that focused on third world population problems.[84] Adherents to this way of thinking have been dubbed "Neo-Malthusians," in reference to Thomas Malthus, who predicted in the late 18th century that population growth, if unchecked, could outstrip means of subsistence.[85]

Much of the early attention focused on India, where population control of this vast and growing nation seemed essential for averting famine and malnutrition. Whereas academics were skeptical that it would be possible to promote contraceptive use among "peasants," birth control advocates were more optimistic. Margaret Sanger, the woman credited with making birth control acceptable in the United States, proved influential in galvanizing support for an international family planning movement. With her firm backing, the International

Planned Parenthood Federation (IPPF) was founded in 1952. In the same year, the Population Council was established by John D. Rockefeller III, and funding from foundations for global fertility control began to flow. By the mid-1950s, many population specialists recognized the importance of bringing birth control directly to low income populations in developing countries, and pilot projects were launched in India and elsewhere.[86]

The 1960s were the years of burgeoning demographic awareness among the general public. The fairly esoteric topic of demographic growth took on new meaning for the U.S. population with the publication of several high profile books: *This Crowded World* (by Osborn) in 1960, followed by Paul Ehrlich's bestseller, *The Population Bomb*, in 1968 and *Famine 1975!* (by Paddock and Paddock) in 1975. These treatises were designed to be alarmist in tone, and Paul Ehrlich and his wife, Ann, went on to advocate the need for incentives bordering on coercion to induce couples to have fewer children. There was also considerable debate on rapid population growth in scholarly circles through much of the period from 1965 to 1975. However, the mainstream population advocates called for *voluntary* family planning. The position among both "birth controllers" and population specialists was that inducing Third World women to practice contraception would simultaneously improve these individuals' social and economic situation *and* alleviate societal problems.[87] The importance of maintaining this focus on both the individual and the collective welfare summarizes the argument of this book.

During the 1960s, the U.S. government became involved in population issues. In 1965, President Lyndon Johnson established population offices in the Department of State and in the United States Agency for International Development (USAID). The first director of the Office of Population at USAID, Dr. Reimert (Ray) Ravenholt, was a charismatic if controversial leader whose bold actions set the agenda for the subsequent implementation of U.S. population programs worldwide. Whereas many development specialists still preached that desired family size was driven almost entirely by *demand factors* (e.g., socioeconomic conditions, levels of education), Ravenholt approached the issue with the less conventional vision that *supply factors* could alter reproductive desires. Specifically, he promoted greater *access to family planning* in countries worldwide, with the idea that the first order of business was to put contraception within the reach of potential users, whether or not they initially expressed interest in using it.

This approach to family planning, which is now almost as commonplace as immunization programs for children, was nonetheless revolutionary at the time. It required that governments take a position on this politically charged issue, which ran counter to the pronatalist cultural norms of many countries. Whereas programs promoting "death control" (decreasing morbidity and mortality, especially among women and children) were politically popular, interventions to promote birth control—when first introduced—did not enjoy the same widespread political and popular acceptance. In sparsely populated countries (e.g., much of Africa), leaders failed to view increased numbers as a problem. In predominantly Catholic countries (e.g., most of Latin America, the Philippines) programs promoting the use of artificial methods of contraception were highly controversial. Since then, the vast majority of Latin countries have chosen to offer family planning services through a combination of government and private programs.

The attempts by the United States to promote family planning overseas in countries not yet "ready" for this message inevitably met with cries of imperialism. Host country officials wondered why the United States was promoting family planning instead of addressing—to their way of thinking—more pressing needs. In part to defuse this issue, the United States worked within the United Nations' system to help create the United Nations Fund for Population Activities (UNFPA)[88] in 1969. By the 1970s, UNFPA served as a major source of funds to population initiatives in developing countries.

The story of international family planning that has unfolded from the 1970s to date is framed by three world population conferences held in 1974, 1984, and 1994.

Three World Conferences on Population: A Curious Evolution

The World Population Conference in Bucharest in 1974 was organized by members of the United Nations in an attempt to bring together government officials from over 100 countries around the world to examine the facts and consequences of rapid population growth. The organizers (primarily from Western countries) expected that developing countries around the world would recognize this as a problem and join a growing movement to curb rapid population growth. To the chagrin of many Western population experts, there was no such endorsement. Rather, the majority of developing nations joined together in stating their overriding preoccupation with the importance of socioeconomic development (in its own right and as a catalyst to lowering fertility) and called for a "New International Economic Order." The position of developing countries at this meeting is captured by a phrase now linked to Bucharest: "development is the best contraceptive."[89]

By the time of the International Conference on Population in Mexico City in 1984, many of these same governments had changed their thinking radically on the issue of family planning. They came to Mexico eager to expand their work in family planning and to develop an agenda that would increase funding from the international donor community. Even in Africa, national programs were being established or gaining strength, thanks in part to a shift in development funding toward the African continent during the 1980s. In a period relatively free from civil strife and before the full impact of the AIDS epidemic, African countries were also seeing the benefits of more widespread family planning programs, if not for demographic reasons, at least for the health of women and children. Asia and Latin America were beginning to show promising results in increasing contraceptive prevalence and lowering fertility rates.

However, it was the United States that was slow in responding at Mexico City. The official U.S. delegation under the administration of President Ronald Reagan asserted that "population is a neutral phenomenon" in the development process and that the excessive state control of the economy was more responsible for economic stagnation than rapid population growth.[90] The U.S. position was curiously at odds with the USAID-funded policy initiatives and programs in the developing countries represented at the meeting. Instead of rallying the world community behind population issues, the United States bestowed upon the world its Mexico City Policy. The U.S. administration, over strong congressional objection, decided to police the actions of developing countries in terms of abortion services by refusing to fund family planning activities of local organizations that also provided abortion, even if legal in that country and paid for by private funds. The position reflected the tensions of a Democratic congress working with a Republican administration. Countries expecting to benefit from the largesse of the donor community in response to their increased commitment to family planning were instead perplexed by this new stipulation. International family planning advocates regretted this lost opportunity but continued to implement an ever-increasing number of programs around the world. Family planning, once a politically taboo and culturally sensitive topic, was becoming a household word, no thanks to the U.S. position in Mexico City.

By 1994, family planning programs had been in operation for 40 years in a few pioneering countries, for 30 years in the majority of developing countries in Asia and Latin America, and for 10 to 20 years in many African nations. During much of this period, the emphasis was on making family planning programs more effective (through voluntary programs in the vast majority of cases, China and, briefly, India being notable exceptions). The driving rationale for family planning continued to focus on its benefits at both the macro and micro levels: for nations (to maintain a balance between population and resources) and for individuals (to enhance the health and well-being of mothers and their children).

The 1994 International Conference on Population and Development (ICPD) in Cairo radically altered the international population movement. The major outcome was a new definition of population policy, which gave prominence to reproductive health while downplaying the demographic rationale for population policy.[91] The so-called common agenda had been carefully crafted by two disparate groups: the feminists and the Neo-Malthusians. The basic tenets of the common agenda were as follows:

- Population stabilization is a desirable, ultimate goal, although not one warranting the use of compulsion.

- National programs enhancing access to contraception are justified in terms of individual human rights, not in terms of their development advantages for aggregate populations.

- The empowerment of women is a prerequisite for the enduring low fertility that population stabilization requires.[92]

The Cairo conference was considered a resounding success since it enabled groups with historically opposing views to identify a unified position and pursue issues that were fundamentally important to them. It gave the feminists at the ICPD an unprecedented platform for championing the importance of gender equity, which in the Cairo declaration became the pathway to lower fertility. At the same time, population advocates could accept the idea of promoting family planning for the benefits it brings to individual women, since increased use of family planning among those women would add to its greater prevalence and lower fertility among the population as a whole. Moreover, many in this group fully embraced the move toward more humane, client-friendly services for women and men of the developing world.

However, as the euphoria of Cairo faded, many of those working in population were taken by surprise that discussion of aggregate trends or demographic concerns became politically incorrect. In some circles, the belief exists that "programs that are demographically driven, and are intended to act directly on fertility, are inherently coercive and abusive of women's right to choose the number and timing of their children."[93] Others would argue that there is nothing inherently abusive or intrusive about demographically driven population policy.[94] Whereas many population advocates looked favorably on the more humanistic approach to family planning that Cairo promised, they had not realized that "buying into Cairo" would mean disavowing any interest in curbing rapid population growth.

"Moderates" on this question are left to wonder why the two sides are being viewed as incompatible (when, in fact, they are not). Wouldn't improving family planning services encourage more women and men to enter a program, adopt a method, and continue sustained contraceptive use? Indeed, one could imagine a win-win situation where better services would mean better treatment of women (consistent with the Cairo agenda) and more sustained contraceptive use (consistent with the demographic objectives of reduced fertility). Just before the Cairo conference, Sinding, Ross, and Rosenfield published a landmark paper, "Seeking Common Ground: Unmet Need and Demographic Goals."[95] This paper reflects the moderate position that by satisfying the unmet need for contraception among women who express an interest in postponing the next birth (including indefinitely), one can achieve greater fertility decline than by setting demographic targets.[96] This rationale reconciles the two camps: those who believe in family planning for the purpose of demographic objectives and those who advocate it for health and reproductive rights alone.

However, there was deep-seated bitterness among feminist groups over what they saw to be male-dominated attempts to control women's reproduction for the demographic objective of lowering fertility. This sentiment caused the pendulum to swing to the other extreme at the ICPD in 1994: downplaying if not downright rejecting the demographic rationale for family planning. Thus, many have interpreted Cairo to mean that family planning should *only* be for the purposes of improving the health and ensuring the reproductive rights of the women who seek out these services. In addition, the ICPD Program of Action called for efforts from governments, community leaders, and citizens to eliminate gender inequality and reinforce men's shared responsibility in reproductive decision making. While the Cairo conference did pay lip service to efforts to reduce population growth and achieve population stabilization, the message from the ICPD was that any demographic benefit that resulted was secondary to the benefit derived from improved services and expansion of women's reproductive rights.

The Politics of Abortion and Its Effect on International Family Planning

Whereas population growth is seemingly a nonpartisan issue, domestic political efforts to associate abortion with international family planning funding have resulted in a battle essentially along party lines in the United States. Unfortunately, this political struggle has greatly affected international family planning funding as politicians strive to uphold their party platforms. Over the past two decades this struggle has intensified, and the attempt to satisfy groups in the United States has resulted in severe consequences internationally.

The efforts of the United States to establish the UNFPA in 1969 and the "New Directions" legislation in 1973 reflected staunch political support of international family planning. Much to the dismay of family planning proponents, however, the influence of more conservative elements began to emerge with the rise of the religious right and its full-blown political emergence in the 1980 presidential election. In response to a growing liberalization regarding a woman's right to an abortion in the United States, the Helms amendment was passed in 1973 prohibiting the use of U.S. government funds for abortion services both in the United States and abroad. USAID continued to fund family planning organizations, including those that supported abortion (with non–U.S. government funds). The Helms amendment marked the start of this bipartisan battle that linked family planning funding and abortion; it was to become the first of many challenges to international family planning funding.

In the wake of *Roe v. Wade* (1973),[97] the anti-abortion forces in the United States began to mobilize and the Right-to-Life factions found allies in the Republican administration of the 1980s. In 1981, the Reagan administration voiced active opposition to abortion and enforced a ban on abortion-related biomedical research and lobbying in the United States. This was followed by the prohibition of the use of public funds for abortion services in the country (42 U.S.C. 300a–6, 1985).[98] These legislative actions were backed by the organized opposition of churches, the growing interest of transnational actors, and the "New Right" conservative leaders.

The Mexico City Policy, announced by the United States at the 1984 International Conference on Population and Development in Mexico, prohibited the funding of international family planning organizations, even with non-U.S. funds, if their programs had any involvement in abortion.[99] Essentially, this policy denied funds to many organizations that the United States had previously supported, including the UNFPA and the IPPF. These larger organizations were generally able to secure funding from private donors to fill this monetary gap; however, many smaller organizations, especially those located abroad, were forced to close their doors. The impact of these cuts was amplified in developing countries where funding had been used to provide not only family planning services but also primary health care.[100]

In addition to the immediate, direct impact the Mexico City Policy had on international family planning funding, there were long-lasting indirect effects. Although abortion research in the United States had declined since 1981, international research continued on this topic. However, with the implementation of the Mexico City Policy, research conducted abroad also waned. Moreover, policy guidelines regarding research programs were extremely ambiguous, and interpretation of the rules could vary greatly. Fear and paranoia ensued; agencies that depended on U.S. funding even began to avoid authorized activities for fear of losing funding.[101] Without the leadership, technological expertise, and financial backing of the United States, many international family planning alliances crumbled, thus hindering the progress of discussion and research. Ironically, despite all the turmoil it caused, the Mexico City Policy did not decrease the incidence of abortion internationally.

From 1985 to 1991, this policy did not change, although pro-life/anti-abortion factions continued to mobilize in the United States. In 1986, the International Right-to-Life Federation was founded and joined with other abortion opponents to ensure the cessation of all U.S. contributions to the UNFPA between 1986 and 1992. This unification, combined with the reaffirmation of the Mexico City Policy by President Bush in 1990, strengthened the position of anti-abortion activists.

During the mid-1980s, domestic and international family planning proponents were much less successful in unifying and lobbying for funds and support. These groups joined forces with international agencies such as the World Health Organization (WHO) and UNICEF to reaffirm the need for adequate family planning support; however, their efforts did not match those of the pro-life advocates.

The Mexico City Policy remained in effect until 1 January 1993, when the newly elected Democratic president, Bill Clinton, took office. The U.S. government restored support to the UNFPA, and USAID resumed support for the IPPF (the largest network of private family planning associations).[102] In addition, international assistance increased markedly in 1994.[103] The change of U.S. administration in 1993 and the Cairo conference in 1994 were vital to the restoration of U.S. funds for international family planning programs.

This success for family planning proponents was short-lived, however, as 1994 marked the establishment of a Republican-dominated Congress for the first time in 39 years and ushered in a "formidable bloc" of anti-abortion conservatives.[104] This conservative faction initiated steps to reinstate the Mexico City Policy, this time in the form of the Smith amendment. The Smith amendment, or what family planning proponents refer to as the "Global Gag Rule," was added to the Foreign Operations Appropriations Bill (H.R. 2159). It sought to deny "U.S. family planning assistance to private organizations overseas if they use other, non-U.S. funds to provide legal abortion services or to participate in policy debates over abortion in their own countries."[105] In 1995, the House of Representatives passed the Smith Amendment (H.R. 1757), despite the opposition of the Senate and President Clinton.

The battle continued in 1996 when Congress mandated a 35 percent cut in U.S. population assistance and stipulated a nine-month delay and metered release of these funds. The international family planning community viewed this as a thinly veiled form of harassment. This year-long 35 percent cut is estimated to have caused 1.9 million unplanned births and 1.6 million abortions, in addition to 8,000 maternal deaths and 134,000 infant deaths.[106] The decreased allotment of funds was eventually released after five months, in February 1997, after President Clinton intervened. Again, this success was tempered by the passage of H.R. 581, the Smith-Oberstar-Hyde Bill, which enacted limitations similar to those of the Mexico City Policy. The passage of this bill may be attributed to the efforts of anti-abortion forces, who

> led by the National Right to Life Committee, the Christian Coalition, Human Life International, the Family Research Council, and the Catholic bishops, waged an all-out disinformation campaign to convince the American public and wavering House members that supporting the March 1 release of population funds without instituting tight, new restrictions to prevent indirect funding of abortion was tantamount to voting in favor of what they called the Clinton Administration's "global abortion crusade."[107]

In recent times, the political repartee continues between Republicans and Democrats regarding the amount and use of family planning funds. The controversy has resulted in severe deadlock, since these funds are linked to other, unrelated UN and International

Monetary Fund monies. Secretary of State Madeleine Albright considers the demands made by some conservative representatives to be "legislative blackmail," since they are withholding other, unrelated funds for the purpose of furthering a moral agenda.[108] This delay has caused anger within both parties, especially considering current political tensions in the Middle East and Eastern Europe. Legislators have "resorted to trading conditions on the timing of the release of population and family planning funding in exchange for a rejection of new policy restrictions."[109] The introduction of highly similar, yet differently worded, bills has attempted to round up moderate Republicans who believe that abortion activities should not be funded but do not want family planning services to suffer (i.e., the Smith-Oberstar-Hyde Bill).

Where Do We Stand?

The international population movement, initiated in the 1950s and popularized during the 1960s, was driven by an "intellectual near-consensus that population growth had to be curbed."[110] A sense of mission pervaded the organizations and individuals working toward this goal. Admittedly, the rapid expansion of family planning programs into uncharted waters and the zeal of some governments to achieve their objectives led to abuses that needed to be exposed and expunged. Indeed, these abuses are at the heart of the feminist rallying cry for more client-oriented, less demographically driven services. Yet the goal remained clear: better health and well-being for individuals, more favorable socioeconomic conditions for the nations with lower fertility, and enhanced prospects of survival for future populations trying to coexist on a planet with finite resources.

Various factors have intervened in the past 20 years to alter the course of the international family planning movement. A series of in-depth analyses of the relationship between population growth and economic development during the 1980s led to revisionist thinking on the extent to which one factor affects the other, thus weakening one of the main arguments in support of international population programs.[111] Evidence of fertility declines in developing countries worldwide led to a belief in some quarters that the problem was "solved," when in fact the vast majority of these countries were continuing to grow at exponential rates. In addition, the AIDS epidemic surfaced in the 1980s, leading many to wonder if it wouldn't be the cruel "solution" to the population problem.

Arguably, the two events that have most altered the course of the international population movement are (1) the spillover of U.S. politics on abortion to the international arena, and (2) the redefinition of population policy in the wake of the Cairo conference. Ironically, there exists an impressive arsenal of technical expertise, contraceptive options, service delivery channels, quality improvement techniques, and communication strategies to deliver family planning worldwide. Yet the purpose of the mission is now less clear.

CHAPTER 7

Determinants of Contraceptive Use and Lower Fertility

Measuring Progress in Family Planning Programs

Many of us can vividly remember the presidency of John F. Kennedy as an event in contemporary history—one that occurred "not too long ago." Yet at the time Kennedy became president (1961), family planning was virtually unknown by the masses in most of the developing world. Over the past 40 years, the world has experienced a contraceptive revolution that few might have believed possible and many Americans still do not realize has occurred at the global level. Family planning has evolved from a politically sensitive, culturally taboo subject to a household word in the majority of developing countries around the world.

The "yardstick" for measuring the success of family planning programs is *contraceptive prevalence*: the percentage of women of reproductive age married or living in union currently using (or whose partner uses) a contraceptive method. As a point of comparison, contraceptive prevalence (including modern and traditional methods) in the United States is 71 percent. China (with the highest reported level in the world) has 83 percent contraceptive prevalence. Mauritania stands in stark contrast with 3 percent.[112]

Some regions of the world have made significantly greater progress in family planning than others (see figure 7.1).[113] The small-family norm that drives contraceptive use took hold far earlier in industrial areas of the world, with the result that prevalence ranges around 70 percent in North America and northern and western Europe. Levels are lower in developing countries, though in some cases they approach those of the industrial world. Despite its Catholic heritage, Latin America boasts a contraceptive prevalence of 67 percent. Asia follows closely behind with 60 percent. But in stark contrast is Africa, with 22 percent.[114]

These regional averages, while instructive, mask dramatic differences within each region between "family planning success stories" and stagnated or fledgling programs. All regions of the world have these contrasts: Asia (with South Korea at 77 percent, Yemen at 7); Latin America (with Costa Rica reporting 75 percent compared to Haiti at 18); and Africa (with Mauritius at 75, Zimbabwe at 48, and Guinea at 2 percent).[115]

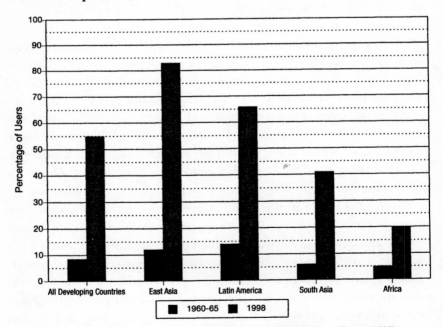

Source: United Nations Population Division (1960–65) and Population Reference Bureau (1998).

Figure 7.1—Trends in Contraceptive Prevalence, by Region

What explains why some countries have had remarkable success with family planning, whereas others lag far behind? In this chapter, we examine the factors that influence the acceptance of family planning.

Factors That Explain Differential Levels of Contraceptive Use

Family planning success (or lack thereof) is best explained as a function of supply and demand, with political support as an overriding factor that influences both.

By *demand*, we refer to the value and demand for children in a given society. A myriad of social, cultural, religious, and legal factors influence the demand for children, and they collectively explain why a woman in sub-Saharan Africa continues to desire six children, while her European counterpart can't be induced to have even two.

The demand for children in turn influences the demand for family planning services. Where couples strive for low fertility, contraceptive services are greatly desired. In contrast, where couples strive to achieve large families, family planning clinics may go unused.

By *supply*, we refer to the "family planning service environment," that is, the organized infrastructure in a given country designed to increase access to contraceptive services. The supply environment is strongly influenced by larger political and economic realities. For example, is there political support for family planning (without which government programs tend to languish)? Is there adequate resource allocation to development programs in general and to family planning in particular? What legal restrictions (on eligibility for obtaining contraceptive methods) or regulatory mechanisms (such as high taxes on contraceptives imported into the country) affect program implementation?

Where the supply environment is strong, family planning tends to be accessible, of high quality (by local standards), and culturally acceptable. On the contrary, a weak supply environment is characterized by a lack of service delivery points offering contraception, poor quality services, and a negative image of family planning as an institution. The forces of supply (of services) and demand (for those services) intersect when a potential client seeks out services. Does she (and most users are indeed women) feel the need for this service, and if so, does she find a source of service that satisfies her need for contraception in the short run and encourages her to continue its use in the long run?

With this as background, we examine political, societal, and individual factors that may serve as barriers in the access and use of family planning services in many countries of the developing world.

POLITICAL WILL

In the early days of the population movement, family planning was considered a low priority and a high political risk in many countries. Especially where population density remained low (such as in much of sub-Saharan Africa), there was minimum perception of the immediate threat to the country's well-being by rapid population growth. In light of previous or ongoing political skirmishes, many leaders equated political strength with population counts. The fast-growing youth population represented potential recruits for future military activity. To compound this situation, the strong cultural norms that bestowed status on women based on family size (especially in Africa) worked against family planning.[116] Except in Asia (where family planning was linked to national development efforts in a number of countries),[117] few politicians wanted to risk the political fallout of openly supporting family planning.

RESOURCE ALLOCATION

In the 1960s and 1970s, much of the funding for family planning came from outside donors, the foremost of which was USAID.[118] However, in recent years the funding allotted to family planning can scarcely meet the growing demand worldwide for this service (due to more youth entering reproductive age and more women and men of reproductive age wanting services). As a result, many countries now cover a sizeable portion of their family planning expenditures from their own budgets (75 percent of the $4 billion spent on family planning).[119] Under this scenario, family planning "competes" with the multitude of other pressing public health needs, including the soaring needs in the area of HIV/AIDS prevention, treatment, and care.

LEGAL CODES AND REGULATIONS

This often-overlooked set of factors can have serious consequences for the functioning of family planning programs. Until recently (the past 10–15 years), many of the African countries previously under French rule labored under the "Law of 1920."[120] This law stipulated that it was illegal to distribute contraceptives or information on fertility control, not unlike the Comstock Act in the United States, which was finally overturned by Congress in 1971.[121] As programs began to develop in these countries, program administrators were understandably cautious in the face of this legal barrier. Most African countries successfully removed it from the books by the late 1980s, and "de facto" it is not practiced in a few countries where "de jure" it still exists. However, this law unquestionably had a dampening effect on family planning promotion to that point.

Similarly, many countries (including some that have achieved fairly high levels of contraceptive prevalence) have rules and regulations at the service delivery level (the so-called medical barriers) that serve to discourage contraceptive use. These rules are often created in an attempt to safeguard users from any negative effects of contraception, but in the process they curtail use unnecessarily. The classic example of this is the "120 rule" for sterilization eligibility, which exists in a number of countries. This rule stipulates that for a woman to be eligible for sterilization, her age multiplied by the number of children she has must equal or exceed 120. (Thus, a 30-year-old woman with four children would be eligible; her 35-year-old counterpart with only three children would not.) These rules were developed to placate the concerned medical community and conservative political factions. In the past decade, international family planning agencies have invested extensive resources in sorting out the valid contraindications to contraceptive use from rules that needlessly deprive clients of desired contraception.[122]

CIVIL UNREST

The political situation in sub-Saharan Africa has wreaked havoc on fledgling family planning programs. For example, Rwanda was making notable progress in increasing access to family planning services when the widespread killings of 1994 brought a halt to "life as normal" in this central African country. In the Democratic Republic of the Congo (formerly Zaire), the national family planning program was steadily expanding when civil strife and President Mobutu's attempt to cling to power caused the international donor community to withdraw all support from development programs, including family planning. Although the clinic structures survived, along with some committed missionaries and locals (whose salaries were unpaid for months at a time), attempts to maintain the program were virtually paralyzed by lack of operational funds.

URBAN/RURAL DIFFERENCES

The degree of urbanization influences fertility desires. In a rural, agrarian setting, children are considered an asset: they offer additional hands to cultivate the fields and take care of household chores. By contrast, in urban settings they become a liability: children require food that must be purchased (not grown in the fields), housing that is scarce, school fees, and transportation to school. Urban families are also exposed to more "modern" ideas through the media. As a result, ideal family size decreases as rural families migrate to the city.

SOCIOECONOMIC FACTORS

The socioeconomic development of a country is a key determinant of contraceptive use.[123] It is no coincidence that industrialized countries have high levels of contraceptive use, whereas the poor nations of the world lag far behind. In part, "rich countries" (including developing countries that have become rich in recent decades) can afford to provide social services, including family planning, to their populations. Moreover, rapid social and economic development reduces the motivation for larger families.[124]

The influence of socioeconomic status on the demand for children has been demonstrated in countries around the world. One of the key variables is education. Studies worldwide have shown that more educated women tend to have fewer children (and thus a greater need for contraception) than their less educated counterparts. (This relationship is weaker in Africa than elsewhere but still evident.[125]) One explanation is that education provides women with alternatives to childbearing as a means of achieving personal satisfaction and social recognition. Another is that education increases their exposure to outside ideas.

THE QUANTITY/QUALITY TRADE-OFF

In view of these social and economic pressures, many couples find themselves confronted with the quantity/quality trade-off.[126] They recognize the need to balance their desires for a large family with the knowledge that fewer children may equate to a higher standard of living in the future. Faced with this trade-off, many opt to limit the number of children in hopes of raising "higher quality" offspring. This is arguably one of the strongest factors that explains the dramatic rise in contraceptive use in "traditional societies" throughout Asia and Latin America and quite probably in the emerging success stories in sub-Saharan Africa (Botswana, Zimbabwe, Kenya).[127] Yet for couples to make this sacrifice, they must feel some assurance that their "investment" in quality children will in fact pay off. In systems where jobs are awarded based on political pull or cronyism, with little value given to educational achievement, parents understandably question the value of this investment. This leads instead to the "lottery ticket mentality": it's better to have a lot of children to increase the odds that one will be a winner.

INFANT/CHILD MORTALITY

Couples in developed countries take the survival of their children for granted. Parents in developing countries, especially those with poor nutritional status and an inadequate health structure, do not have this luxury. High infant mortality rates result in the tendency to anticipate the worst, leading to "additional births" to ensure the survival of at least some children to adulthood. No population in the developing world has experienced a sustained fertility reduction without first having a major decline in infant and child morbidity.[128]

STATUS OF WOMEN

Our Western experience provides us with little appreciation for the extent to which the status of women in some developing countries dictates their fertility behavior. While this broad generalization hardly applies to the women on the beaches in Rio de Janeiro, it has staggering implications for women in countries where their potential is dictated by their gender. The vicious cycle begins in infancy, when female babies may receive less nourishment and medical care than their male siblings. When they reach school age, girls are more likely to be kept at home while boys go to school; or if allowed to begin, girls may be withdrawn at a far earlier age. By 14 or 15 years old, they are considered marriageable. In societies where a woman's worth is measured in terms of childbearing, the one viable option is to begin having children.

The role of the woman as a "baby factory" emerged in particularly poignant fashion in focus groups conducted in the mid-1980s in the Democratic Republic of the Congo. Participants explained that if a woman needed to have a tubal ligation for medical reasons, then her husband (and family) would often be supportive of the decision. Yet as soon as she couldn't produce more children, her husband's family might convince him to take another woman.[129]

RELIGION

The role of religion in fertility and family planning is complex. It is often the source of amazement to many that family planning has made such dramatic inroads in Latin America, where over 90 percent of the population purports to be Catholic. Similarly, one sometimes hears that Islam is a deterrent to contraceptive use, yet several predominantly Muslim countries (such as Indonesia and Morocco) have had very successful family planning programs. Does religion play a role or not?

The evidence suggests that religion is less important than other factors (such as economic motivations, the quantity/quality trade-off) in determining the demand for children and, in turn, contraceptive use. However, religion becomes an important factor when government and religious leaders join to oppose family planning. Bolivia in the 1970s and 1980s is a good example. The Catholic Church, in collaboration with government officials, successfully curbed the import of contraceptives to Bolivia. While the contraceptive revolution took hold in neighboring countries of Latin America, Bolivia had one of the lowest levels of contraceptive prevalence on the continent. Yet "where there's a will, there's a way," as reflected by the statistics on contraceptive prevalence. Despite more open policies toward contraceptive service delivery in Bolivia in recent years, only 18 percent of married women use a modern contraceptive method; yet another 27 percent use a "traditional method" (such as rhythm or withdrawal),[130] reflecting the strong desire on the part of this population to regulate fertility, whether or not the government is willing to help.

Religion may also play a role in the contraceptive methods selected. For example, in certain Catholic countries (e.g., the Philippines), a substantial proportion of users rely on rhythm, a method sanctioned by the Catholic Church. Islamic nations may promote family planning but show ambivalence toward permanent methods (whereas in the majority of "successful" family planning programs, voluntary sterilization is often the leading method). Examples include Indonesia and Morocco; both have a prevalence rate in the mid-50s, but only 8 percent of users have opted for sterilization. This contrasts strongly with a number of Latin American countries where over half of all contraceptive use is sterilization: Dominican Republic (69 percent), El Salvador (59 percent), and Panama (56 percent).

CULTURAL/ETHNIC FACTORS

Additional factors—often foreign to Western thinking—work to promote strongly pronatalist practices. One such factor is ethnic identity. All regions of the developing world have ethnic minorities that for historical reasons have rejected family planning. Guatemala—with the lowest level of contraceptive prevalence in Central America (31 percent)—is a case in point. Whereas the Spanish-speaking majority, representing some 50–60 percent of the total population, has largely accepted family planning (the prevalence among Ladinos [Spanish-speaking Guatemalans of mixed ancestry] is 43 percent), the various Mayan groups that constitute the rest of the country's population have only a 10 percent prevalence.[131]

In numerous African countries, the issue of ethnic group equates directly with the importance of the clan.[132] Individuals feel a great debt to their ancestors and feel a moral obligation to repay those who have gone before them. One very direct and concrete means of doing so is to add to the numbers of the clan. To refuse to procreate would be selfish.

"Beyond Family Planning": Incentives

To understand the evolution of family planning (and some of the history behind the arguments of women's groups at the Cairo conference), it is important to consider the role of incentives and disincentives in family planning programs. In the early days of family planning, those impatient to achieve lower fertility considered incentives as an expedient means to an end (and indeed, China and others have demonstrated that they can be effective). Today, with near universal consensus that family planning programs should be voluntary, incentives are viewed as an undesirable vestige of the past. However, cash incentives for sterilization are reported to persist in Bangladesh, India, Nepal, Pakistan, and Sri Lanka.[133]

In the 1950s, India was the first country to introduce incentives to influence childbearing behavior; subsequently, a number of nations followed suit by either rewarding citizens for compliance with policy or punishing them for going against it. In total, 29 countries had incorporated incentives into their family planning programs by 1980, 16 of the countries being in Asia.[134]

Incentives were targeted to three different groups: *acceptors* (women and men complying with the government family planning policy), *providers* (physicians and other health care providers), and *promoters* (individuals within the community who influenced the acceptors to adopt the family planning policy). Payment was usually in the form of cash for the providers and cash, services, or gifts to the acceptors and promoters.[135] For example, in India, men and women received gifts in the form of traditional garments, radios, and money for undergoing sterilization, and men were duly compensated for expenses and time lost from work.[136] In China, incentives have included monthly welfare, and nutritional allowances, as well as priorities in housing, education, and medical care.

A number of countries experimented with payments to promoters and providers. Doctors in Sri Lanka, Pakistan, Taiwan, and Turkey received money for reaching the specified number of intrauterine device (IUD) insertions per month. On the community level, promoters in Thailand and the Philippines were paid small commissions for the sale of contraceptives to women.[137]

In addition to using incentives as a means to encourage family planning, many countries have used disincentives to increase compliance with national childbearing and birth spacing policies. Disincentives usually include a revocation of benefits and/or fines for each child in excess of the stated policy. In some circumstances, failure to comply with government policy resulted in loss of employment, especially for providers and promoters.[138]

In Singapore, a family planning program was initiated in the late 1960s, shortly after the nation's independence. Entitled "Two Is Enough," the program focused on changing fertility behavior and decreasing the population growth rate through the implementation of disincentives. Public hospitals increased delivery fees for each additional child, restrictions were placed on the choice of schools for third or successive children, and maternity leave was withdrawn from couples having more than two children.[139] Disincentives have also been used as part of China's population policy.

Ethical considerations aside, incentives have been successful in lowering fertility rates. The incentives are considered to be a factor (along with the provision of free or low cost contraceptives) contributing to the decrease in the total fertility rate in Asia from 5.7 in 1970 to 2.9 in 1992.[140] In Singapore, the population growth rate dropped from 2.3 percent to 1.3 percent in the 10-year period from 1968 to 1978. Ironically, fertility rates in Singapore are now below replacement level, prompting the government to organize a commission to devise ways to bring singles together in the 1990s.[141] A back-to-work program has also been introduced to support women. Similarly, South Korea and Malaysia have both adopted incentive programs to increase the number of children per household.

The use of incentives directly violates the spirit of voluntary family planning because it deprives a woman or couple of determining freely the number and timing of their children. Also, incentives have been linked to abuses of human rights. For example, in the 1970s, India not only provided incentives to individuals but also penalized officials for not reaching assigned quotas. Problems arose when public officials allegedly used force on low-status individuals to meet their quotas. This in turn created a backlash, contributing to the defeat of Indira Gandhi's government, and setbacks for family planning in India.[142]

Recognizing the unethical use of coercion, few countries still employ incentives or disincentives, which have ultimately been found to harm or punish women and families (e.g., the nth child, the poor, and racial and ethnic minorities). During the 1994 International Conference on Population and Development, the use of coercion through incentives was condemned, and for the first time demographic targets were abandoned.[143] Instead the emphasis has been placed on allowing individual choice when determining family size, in addition to raising awareness regarding women's reproductive health, creating greater access to education, increasing employment opportunities, and improving access to health care. However effective incentives may have been in the past in selected countries, they are not viewed as part of the arsenal to be used in confronting rapid population growth in the 21st century.

Available Options

Outsiders to the population field often imagine that promoting family planning in developing countries is "doomed to failure." Many have heard about the debacles that have tarnished the record of international family planning: persuading men in India to have vasectomies in exchange for transistor radios and, more recently, sterilizing women in Peru without their consent. They point to the high fertility rates of Africa as "proof" that family planning does not work in developing countries. They assume that family planning would never take hold in the Catholic countries of Latin America.

In fact, family planning programs have been highly effective in reducing fertility in countries with favorable socioeconomic conditions and strong delivery systems for family planning services. A number of developing countries in the world (or recent "graduates") now have contraceptive prevalence levels similar to or higher than in the United States: China, Korea, Taiwan, Thailand, Costa Rica, and Mauritius. Moreover, there is evidence (from Bangladesh) that family planning can gain widespread acceptance even in countries with low socioeconomic conditions if there is strong political will and a high level of access to services. The field has learned a great deal over the past three decades about the delivery of services, not only in the clinic setting but also by community health workers (known as "community-based distribution") and through social marketing programs. In this sense, we know how to get the job done.

We have three options with regard to the continued high level of population growth in the vast majority of countries.

STRATEGY #1: PROMOTE LOWER FERTILITY

The service delivery mechanisms needed to increase access to family planning programs are in place in the vast majority of developing countries. Moreover, the small-family norm has become so deeply ingrained in a number of countries that even if the public-sector family planning infrastructure disappeared, contraceptive prevalence would probably remain high; that is, couples would be sufficiently motivated to find other sources of contraception.

In addition, the current focus on increasing the quality of services attracts new users and maintains existing users in the program (or at least using contraception). Even programs that disavow any interest in demographic objectives may in fact be working toward lowered fertility by providing a constellation of reproductive health services (including contraception) for women and men of reproductive age.

Contraception is not the only means of influencing fertility. Indeed, there are three other "proximate determinants of fertility": age at marriage (a proxy for exposure to the risk of pregnancy), postpartum insusceptibility to pregnancies, and incidence of abortion.[144] In many developing countries, the first two are undergoing changes but in ways that tend to cancel each other out. That is, due to socioeconomic progress and the changing status of women in many countries, women are seeking greater educational opportunities and postponing marriage. Although this does not necessarily preclude their exposure to pregnancy, single women do have a lower risk than married women in almost all countries of the world. Some countries have attempted to "manipulate" these variables for demographic purposes (e.g., increasing the age of marriage in China to 22 for men and 20 for women in 1980).[145] Because of the forces of modernization and exposure to outside ideas, the practice of prolonged breastfeeding is on the wane in most countries. Although breastfeeding does not guarantee that a particular woman will be protected from pregnancy, the practice tends to delay the resumption of menstruation and thus fecundity among breastfeeding women on the whole. In short, women decrease their likelihood of pregnancy by remaining unmarried, but they increase it by abandoning the practice of prolonged breastfeeding. However, compared to contraception, these two factors account for far less of the variance in fertility rates and thus do not qualify as factors to be addressed in most intervention programs.

The final means of lowering fertility is induced abortion. This practice is legal in selected countries of the world (Tunisia, Barbados, Vietnam, Singapore, as well as in the United States and most European countries). It is illegal, however, in the majority of nations, though the practice exists surreptitiously in most countries. Even where legal, abortion is not promoted for demographic reasons (though the opposite was true in Romania when Ceausescu prohibited the use of abortion in 1966 to stimulate birth rates;[146] it worked well when people were initially taken by surprise with this policy, but over time they were able to discover alternative means of controlling fertility).

In summary, contraception remains the one most powerful tool available to developing countries for lowering fertility and stabilizing population growth rates.

STRATEGY #2: TOLERATE INCREASED MORTALITY

This "solution" is unacceptable. Most countries of the world and development agencies are committed to sustaining life. The occasional so-called ethnic cleansings that occur, to the horror of the world community, are targeted at decreasing the numbers of particular groups, but for political, not demographic, reasons.

In a few countries, AIDS will reduce population growth to close to zero (e.g., 0.2–0.3 percent). Increased mortality rates result in lower life expectancy and a closing of the gap between the number of births and deaths. It is hard to conceive of countries in which one in three adults in urban areas is already affected by HIV and has no access to the lifesaving drugs available in the West. When the AIDS epidemic first surfaced, many asked if this would not effectively spell the end to rapid population growth in Africa (and other affected countries). Indeed, AIDS has lowered the population growth rate in a number of African countries, but all continue to increase in absolute numbers, as detailed in chapter 9. However, the reduction in growth rates due to AIDS is occurring *despite* the best efforts of the public health community, not because of them.

STRATEGY #3: LET NATURE TAKE ITS COURSE

This alternative summarizes the position taken by those who favor a laissez-faire approach to continued population growth. Indeed, because of the existing family planning infrastructure worldwide, a certain amount of contraceptive use will continue, even if all support from the donor community were withdrawn today. However, this approach would result in higher levels of population growth in the long run.

In view of the above, it is important to consider what *can* be done in different countries around the world. In the next chapter we review the actions needed to achieve lower fertility at the global level.

CHAPTER 8

Promoting Lower Fertility in the Post-Cairo Era

The Cairo conference was heralded by most of the population community in the West as a resounding success. A half-decade later, there is widespread interest in "Cairo +5" (referring to progress made toward the Cairo agenda in the subsequent five years), and organizations are working to amass documentation on the progress made in reproductive health since 1994. Unquestionably, important gains have been made in improving the quality of services, integrating the prevention of sexually transmited disease (STD) and HIV into family planning, extending services to include adolescents and men, improving the conditions for safe motherhood, among others. These are truly laudable accomplishments that deserve to be showcased. However, the documentation is unlikely to reflect the other legacy of Cairo:

- The Cairo conference has effectively silenced those who advocate slowing population growth by redefining "acceptable family planning" to address the reproductive rights of individual women, not the interests of nations in curbing population growth. The "compromise" position adopted at Cairo promoted empowerment of women as the pathway to lower fertility rates. Indeed, the implementation of the Cairo agenda has followed the pattern of the

Cairo Plan of Action: little explicit mention of population stabilization as a final outcome.

- Many people remain unconvinced—and indeed there is little scientific evidence to indicate—that improving the health and social condition of women will have a demographic impact.[147] As Tsui states, "No exacting set of research findings exists to underwrite the expectations that improved reproductive and sexual health will prompt couples to exercise their reproductive choices in a manner that maintains fertility decline, and thereby slows population growth."[148]

- Many agencies and foundations previously concerned by the demographic predicament of the planet in the 20th century have enthusiastically adopted the Cairo agenda. In some cases, this represents genuine endorsement of the new paradigm, whereby individual reproductive rights and women's empowerment are the priority concerns to be addressed. In other cases, it may reflect political expediency: agencies wishing to pursue the goal of increased contraceptive use worldwide have redefined their programs to conform to the new approach. As a consequence of this far-reaching shift from family planning toward reproductive health, it now seems that to be pro-Cairo requires cutting one's ideological ties with past interest in demographic trends.

- Two major agencies that defined the population agenda in the past—USAID and UNFPA—have retained population stabilization as an agency goal,[149] yet many of their front-line staff are reluctant to emphasize this aspect of their portfolio for fear of seeming politically incorrect or "anti-Cairo." Within the UNFPA there is uncertainty as to how to define the agency's primary objectives.[150] Public statements reflect the skittishness over its position. For example, the 1996 UNFPA report of the Secretary General seems to skirt the issue of fertility goals by stating that "population issues are more than just demographic concerns."[151]

- Many of the senior members of the international population community have found themselves alienated from their own profession. The group of professionals who entered the field in the late 1960s and 1970s in the belief that the world would be a better place if population growth could be curbed through voluntary family planning find their "cause" outdated, irrelevant, and/or suspect. Although they hold top-level jobs in their respective organizations and are positioned to make a major contribution in terms of resource allocation and technical input, many feel a sense of disorientation in the wake of the Cairo conference. A goal to which they have dedicated the better part of their professional lives has been devalued.

- The sudden disavowal of demographic goals has thrown family planning programs and personnel into some disarray.[152] Governments in many developing countries struggle to implement the Cairo agenda with shrinking financial support from the West. The rhetoric of Cairo did not bring a long-term increase in funding levels for the expanded range of reproductive health services. Thus, the message to governments (confronted with deteriorating economies, growing civil unrest, and the burgeoning AIDS epidemic, to mention a few of the challenges) has been to do more with less. Some have succeeded impressively (see the description of Mexico, below). For others, "implementing Cairo" has not been easy.

- There is the very real possibility of a "lose-lose" situation that could result from inadequate funding in this area. As a consequence of the decision to drop the demographic rationale, senior policymakers who make the macro-economic resource allocation decisions in governments and donor agencies may cut back support for reproductive health/family planning programs. The ironic result could be significantly fewer services for women and deterioration in women's health status.[153]

For those who believe that the goal of curbing population growth remains a top priority, what should be the call to action? In this chapter we outline seven key points.

1. *The international population community needs to exert leadership on the issue of population growth.*

To avoid seeming "anti-Cairo," many senior population officials have shied away from discussion of population growth. If asked directly whether population is still an important issue, they would agree. Yet they pursue the path of least resistance in their daily lives, which is to promote family planning for the good of women. In their own minds, they have not compromised their original ideals because they continue to pursue actions that make family planning more readily available to women (and men) in need of it around the world. Yet the sense of purpose has waned.

The field needs high-level spokespersons to make the case that curbing population growth and improving individual reproductive welfare are not incompatible goals. In fact, this is the argument that Sinding et al. make when they demonstrate that satisfying the level of unmet need (reported by women in national-level studies worldwide) would have a greater demographic impact than would trying to achieve the demographic targets set by selected countries.[154]

USAID articulates this principle with one of its major initiatives "Maximizing Access and Quality," which crosscuts many of its field projects. A basic premise behind this philosophy is that increasing the quality of care (making services more responsive to the individual needs and interests of clients) will have the double benefit of improving quality for its own sake *and* attracting/retaining a greater number of users of contraceptive methods. Whereas it is politically correct to discuss "access" (which benefits the individual by making services more convenient), it still seems "anti-Cairo" to mention the macro-level importance of access: to increase coverage of family planning services, essential for demographic impact.

In recent years the environmental movement has become more vocal about the effects of population growth on world resources, and many people have called for renewed efforts toward "population control." (In the population field, this term has strongly negative connotations, even among those who favor curbing population growth, because of past abuses involving coercion, incentives, and targets.) Ironically, population advocates find themselves in the awkward position of embracing this potential alliance while trying to explain that family planning is no longer about curbing population growth.

2. *The public must realize that the population problem is still "alive and well."*

In the mid-1970s when the first signs of decreases in fertility rates in several developing countries were reported in the media, there was a widespread misperception that the population problem was "solved." Lost in the debate were two important considerations: (1) that the population growth rate can be declining, but as long as it remains positive, growth will continue (though at a slower pace), and (2) that even when a country attains replacement-level fertility, growth can continue for 50–60 years more (if youth represent a disproportionate segment of the population, as is the case in most developing countries today).

To add to the "honest error" of the media, a series of articles has been published proclaiming that growth—even if it continues to occur—is *beneficial* to society. Ben Wattenberg has received widespread publicity for his book entitled *The Birth Dearth*, which makes this argument. The late Julian Simon championed the benefits of population as a means of continuously enriching the knowledge base from which we can address the problems of declining renewable resources.[155] While all are entitled to an opinion, these arguments allowed the U.S. public to dismiss population growth as one less problem they have to deal with. And given the ambivalence among population experts to openly focus on population growth, lest they be branded "anti-Cairo," efforts on their part to educate the media on these issues have fallen off. Of note, the *National Geographic* (not known as a hotbed of political dialogue) has been one exception to the silence of the media on the issue of population. The October 1998 issue opens with the statement that "Of all the issues we face as the new millennium nears, none is more important than population growth."[156] It spotlights the realities of continued population growth with graphics and visuals that few academic publications could match.

The millennium will cause many to pause and take stock of where we have been and where we are going. The population community needs to ensure that the demographic issue remains visible in the 21st century.

3. *Donors must champion the collective good in addition to the individual benefits of family planning and reproductive health.*

The Cairo conference was a useful catalyst in drawing attention to issues of gender equity and women's empowerment. Most in the social development business consider this an important component in improving the social condition of the world's population. Thus, this newly placed emphasis on "neglected areas" is seen in a positive light. To cite two examples, the International Planned Parenthood Federation developed and implemented its Vision 2000,[157] which spotlights the sexual and reproductive health needs of women and adolescents (one of which is access to contraception). The Rockefeller Foundation developed a portfolio of operations research projects in the "more neglected" areas of south Asia and sub-Saharan Africa to encourage local organizations to identify and test ways to deliver services to adolescents, implement postabortion services, and expand STD/HIV/AIDS prevention services. These initiatives are to be applauded as part of the new emphasis on meeting the reproductive health needs of individuals, especially women, in developing countries. Yet such initiatives should not be seen as inconsistent with parallel efforts to increase access and have impact at the population level.

In July 1998, Dr. Nafis Sadik, executive director of the UNFPA, issued a statement to commemorate World Population Day. In it, she discussed the need for bringing family planning services to developing countries in the world as a means of promoting a better life for all in the future. Given the prominent role of the UNFPA in Cairo, her message seems almost at odds with what has been the "interpretation" of Cairo in the past five years (de-emphasizing the benefits of family planning at the aggregate level). Yet this brief message, shown on television around the world, exemplifies what other leaders in this field need to communicate: curbing population growth is still an important goal; the tag line should be "and we can do it with client-friendly services."

4. *Governments should be encouraged to simultaneously promote lower fertility and improved services.*

As this book goes to press, there is much discussion of "Cairo+5." This series of meetings and events has refocused attention on the question of what governments have done to implement the expansion of reproductive health services in their own countries. Cairo deserves credit as the catalyst for stimulating action in three areas in particular: the integration of HIV/AIDS prevention into family planning services, the development and expansion of reproductive health services for adolescents (now a priority among donors and governments worldwide), and an increased investment in the education of girls.

Yet this attention does not have to be at the expense of sustained interest in demographic trends. Mexico illustrates a country in which two sets of priorities have been pursued simultaneously.[158] As is widely documented, the Mexican government made a historic reversal of its pronatalist policies in the early 1970s and embarked on an aggressive family planning initiative. Four branches of the public sector (CONAPO, SSA, IMSS, and ISSSTE)[159] were enlisted to implement this strategy. In addition, this family planning initiative received important support from two private sector establishments: MEXFAM (the IPPF affiliate) and FEMAP.[160] The success of this initiative has been impressive, with the total fertility rate dropping from an average of 6.5 children from 1970–1975[161] to 2.9 in 1998. Yet consistent with the Cairo agenda, Mexico has embarked on a new set of initiatives designed to improve the quality of care in its family planning services, develop service delivery strategies to attract adolescents, and promote breastfeeding. The Mexican public sector program suffers from none of the cloudy thinking that has characterized some of the post-Cairo efforts. Service providers at all levels are extremely clear regarding the importance of family planning to the welfare of the country as a whole and to the families of individual clients.

In no way has Mexico backed away from its commitment to curb rapid population growth. Rather, it has grafted the Cairo agenda onto its existing service delivery system in ways that further dignify and enhance the program. One example is the country's enthusiastic participation in the UNICEF initiative to credential hospitals that earn it with the title of "Mother and Baby-friendly," which has succeeded in making better health care delivery a priority in Mexico. A second example is the effort to attract and meet the needs of adolescents: by recruiting and training youth-friendly staff, dedicating space to this activity, and strengthening referral processes to other services in these facilities. The results of these efforts leave one to marvel how the Mexican government has succeeded in designing and implementing such forward-looking programs in a country that is predominantly Catholic and restrictive regarding the sexual behavior of young, unmarried women. Moreover, it has maintained financial support for these programs even in times of economic crisis.

5. *Programs must integrate STD/HIV/AIDS prevention into family planning.*

Currently, HIV/AIDS continues to spread rampantly with no cure in sight. Although vaccine trials are underway and drug therapies have become available to prolong the lives of HIV-infected individuals who can afford the prohibitive cost, control of AIDS in developing countries remains a major challenge.

The reaction to integrating HIV/AIDS prevention with family planning services varies by country, depending in large part on the magnitude of the epidemic in a given country. In the handful of sub-Saharan countries where over a quarter of "low-risk" adults (the general public) in urban areas are infected with the HIV virus, the integration of services seems not only logical but imperative. In low HIV prevalence countries, by contrast, program administrators may question the cost-benefit of incorporating this type of counseling and prevention as a routine part of family planning service delivery. In short, the urgency of the AIDS epidemic, combined with the call for a wider range of reproductive health services consistent with women's needs, has led to renewed efforts toward integrating STD/HIV/AIDS prevention into family planning services.

Several compelling arguments are made in favor of integration of services. Untreated STDs are a cofactor in the transmission of HIV; that is, individuals with STDs are at a higher risk of becoming infected with HIV if they have sexual relations with an infected person.[162] The clientele for family planning is women (and some men) who by definition are sexually active and thus potentially at risk, especially in high HIV prevalence countries. In this sense, the infrastructure is in place to reach this group of sexually active adults, and the integration of services optimizes the use of scarce resources.[163] Clients benefit from "one-stop shopping" that decreases their travel time and expenses. In addition, the educational messages from one program reinforce those of the other (e.g., incorporating condoms into sexual relationships is effective in the prevention of STD/HIV and unwanted pregnancy). Finally, it has been argued that combining education, access to condoms, and STD control leads to greater efficiency in the delivery of both HIV/AIDS prevention and family planning services.[164]

However, this integration is not without obstacles. The family planning community struggled for two decades to "sanitize" the image of condoms, which were stigmatized because of their association with illicit sex, especially with prostitutes. AIDS prevention messages bring this association back to light (e.g., wide-reaching media campaigns that promote condom use, especially with "nonregular partners").[165] Similarly, there are fears that using family planning clinics to provide STD treatment to commercial sex workers would drive off the primary clients—married women.

One must also consider the financial implications of integrating these two types of services as STD diagnosis and treatment requires a substantial initial investment.[166] The time and money required for integrated program startup can delay activities and render them less effective than vertical programs (STD/HIV prevention only).[167] In addition, the increased cost of these programs can make finding funds difficult as resources will be needed for not just one but two methods in resource-strained circumstances. (For this reason, despite years of effort to integrate different preventive services, the HIV/AIDS campaign began as a vertical program on the rationale that the magnitude of the problem required resources to be targeted specifically to this problem.)

Perhaps the single largest objection is the "contraceptive trade-off" dilemma: the method that works best for HIV prevention (the condom) is one of the least effective (and least acceptable) for pregnancy prevention. To this we add the problem of "anti-synergy": couples using a method effective for preventing pregnancy may be less likely to use a second method effective in the prevention of STDs.[168]

With AIDS a grim reality for the foreseeable future, governments must act to protect the lives of their citizens. Cynics might suggest that population advocates ("Neo-Malthusians") would do better to let nature take its course if curbing population growth is so important. Yet curbing growth is not an end in itself; the welfare and survival of the world's population is. To this end, family planning programs must expand to do their part in the fight against AIDS.

6. *We must continue to invest in the education of women.*

Here the feminists and population advocates tend to agree. Education is a cornerstone to improving the status of women worldwide, both for the personal benefits of self-realization that it brings and the skill set it provides for gaining entry to the labor force. Moreover, education is one of the strongest determinants of contraceptive use (and by extension, smaller family size) of any socioeconomic variable in the social science data bank.

As Bongaarts points out, educated women are better able to control their lives, and they have superior knowledge of fertility regulation methods and sources of supply than their less educated counterparts. As a consequence, investments in family planning programs produce larger reductions in unwanted fertility when social conditions, such as education and gender equality, are favorable.[169] To educate women is to improve the life chances of individuals and to advance the development prospects of whole nations.[170] Yet even here there are caveats. As Knodel and Jones have argued,

While the strong emphasis on eliminating gender inequality in schooling is appropriate educational policy in some regions and countries, it is far less pertinent across a wide swathe of countries where such a gender gap is modest or nonexistent. . . .

. . . There is another gap, with serious implications for development and for equality of opportunity, as well as for demographic outcomes, that is largely ignored by this new population policy paradigm: . . . the gap in access to education by socioeconomic status.

By placing the almost sole emphasis on gender inequality, demographers risk aligning themselves with a reactionary perspective that fails to emphasize the urgent need to remove obstacles to greater socioeconomic equity in access to schooling.[171]

Another area relates to the *source of funding* for women's education. Whereas population advocates tend to support this important investment, they are not enthusiastic about using funds earmarked for family planning/reproductive health to this end. They argue that funding is already too limited to effectively implement the family planning services needed worldwide and that the interests of increased contraceptive use are not served if funds are taken away from service delivery for investment in education.

7. *We need to capitalize on the knowledge accumulated over four decades to implement effective family planning programs.*

The world community of family planning specialists—decision makers, program managers, service providers, donor agency staff, program evaluators—has accumulated a wealth of knowledge about the successful implementation of family planning programs.[172] Four decades of field experience, combined with systematic testing of different strategies of contraceptive service delivery, have produced an impressive arsenal of technical know-how for implementing family planning programs. The failures have also been instructive. While new strategies may continue to surface, the current ones are highly adequate for delivering contraception in the majority of developing countries. Although the mechanisms are available, the success in implementing them requires political will and adequate financial resources. We must use what we already know about the successful implementation of programs to guide our future course of action.

- *Family planning flourishes where there is strong political commitment and program leadership.*

Most family planning programs need political support to survive.[173] Where family planning has flourished, there is often an influential leader who has been able to give his or her full, public commitment to family planning. Key examples include Mexico, Thailand, Indonesia, and Zimbabwe, to name a few. Interestingly, the existence of an explicit population policy does not guarantee effective action, as the case of Pakistan illustrates; similarly, Ghana was one of the first African nations to develop an explicit population policy, though it had little effect at the time. In some countries where the government has been unwilling to take a strong stance on the population issue, the local IPPF affiliate has filled this void very effectively (such as in the case of Colombia, considered one of the success stories for family planning). However, the general rule holds that political commitment at the highest level remains a key ingredient to a successful national program.

Another key to successful programs is strong, stable program leadership. This quality of leadership often eludes the quantitative measurement tools of evaluation specialists. Yet there is widespread agreement within the field that strong leadership is vital to successful programs. Dynamic leaders "make inadequate resources do more than anyone can reasonably expect."[174]

- *Increasing access to family planning services positively affects both supply and demand.*

Making contraception more available to clients (the supply side) gives them the means to act on their reproductive intentions. This is a sine qua non for increasing levels of contraceptive use and reducing fertility. However, it also affects the *demand* for contraception. The very presence of contraceptive services in a community stimulates discussion (often negative at first) that serves to inform persons of the existence of products to regulate fertility. Ironically, the sermons preached against family planning from the pulpits of local Catholic churches in Latin America may have had the unintentional result of educating thousands of potential clients about their availability. The mere knowledge that fertility regulation is possible may cause couples to re-evaluate their options, especially those who had considered no other course than continued childbearing.

- *Better services attract more clients and increase continuation rates.*

    Quality of care has become a prime concern for family planning programs in the 1990s. Although there was talk of the user-perspective in the early 1980s, the focus on more client-oriented services has been particularly strong in the past decade. Some argue for improved quality of care for its own sake, consistent with the Cairo message that women of the world deserve to be served with dignity and respect. Others see the benefits of improved quality of services as a means of increasing the numbers of family planning clients and promoting more sustained use of contraception, both of which contribute to increased contraceptive prevalence and lower fertility. Whereas much of the talk about quality of care during the 1980s was just that—talk—many programs have taken action to improve quality and to make themselves accountable to this goal with routine monitoring. Although the empirical evidence of a cause-and-effect relationship between quality of care and increased contraceptive use is still sparse (notable exceptions being Mensch in Peru and El-Zanaty and Associates in Egypt[175]), the field has embraced this push toward quality in a way that is both consistent with Cairo and likely to pay off in more widespread contraceptive use at the population level.

- *Contraceptives are most accessible when multiple mechanisms are used.*

    One of the major constraints to the more widespread use of contraceptives during the 1970s was the reliance on clinic-based services. This type of facility was often located in cities or large towns, leaving those in rural areas without access. Moreover, the expense of a clinic visit (even when heavily subsidized) and the time lost from other activities discouraged many from using these facilities. In response, two alternative strategies have emerged to satisfy the needs of a larger number of potential clients: social marketing[176] and community-based distribution (CBD).[177]

Social marketing treats the "product" as it would any commercially produced item (with the difference that the costs in this case are generally subsidized by the government or external funding agency). The four Ps of marketing are carefully analyzed to determine the most effective: Product (item to be promoted), Price (level affordable to the target population), Place (channels to reach the intended audience), and Promotion (advertising strategy to be used).[178] The packaging and brand names are developed through market research to appeal to preferences and tastes in a particular culture. (For example, the brand name "Pearl" has proven popular for oral pills in many countries: the name connotes beauty and purity, and the pill resembles a pearl in color and shape.) Customers enjoy the convenience of purchasing these products in retail outlets without the long waits associated with a clinic visit. Moreover, they often consider such products superior to the contraceptives available free of charge from government facilities (believing that "you get what you pay for"), even when the chemical composition is identical. And many prefer the status that accompanies being a paying customer, not a recipient of free government services. Social marketing programs have become particularly valuable in those countries where a high percentage of women use methods requiring resupply, such as the pill. They also represent an important means of transferring clients from public sector programs (supported by the government) to private sector programs (where the client assumes some if not all of the cost). For example, converting users from the public to the private sector was an explicit objective of the Indonesian programs in the 1990s. Limitations of this approach include its urban focus (where retail outlets are located), the "commercialism" that some find repugnant for a "social product," and a lack of counseling in this type of commercial transaction.

A second important mechanism for delivering family planning services is CBD. This strategy involves establishing contraceptive depots or CBD posts in areas too remote for residents to have access to clinic-based services or retail outlets selling contraceptives. Alternatively, they may be established in densely populated low-income urban areas to facilitate access. An individual (generally with no formal clinical training) is recruited and trained in the basic aspects of contraceptive service delivery for two or three methods: the pill, condoms, and/or spermicides. (More recently, some programs have experimented with injectables, provided the CBD worker has the necessary technical competence.) He or she is trained to use a checklist to identify contraindications (for the pill) that would make it necessary to instead refer the client to a clinical facility. A supervisor visits periodically to resupply the CBD worker, provide technical input on questions that arise, and, in general, provide motivation for continued participation in the program. The advantages of this system is that it brings contraception to the doorsteps of men and women in remote areas, communities have a ready source of information and referral to other services, and workers (especially women) gain recognition and respect from serving their communities. However, CBD is not without its detractors. This approach to service delivery often meets with strong criticism in its initial phase from local medical societies, whose territorial interests are violated by having someone else in the community authorized to provide contraception (especially pills). These programs tend to be expensive on a per capita basis (especially since CBD generally operates in rural communities with lower population density and less demand for contraception). High levels of turnover (given the low pay, if there is any at all) also lessen the effectiveness of CBD programs.

- *Increased contraceptive choice increases user satisfaction with the methods.*[179]

The world still awaits "the perfect contraceptive." However, most in the population community have come to the realization that it is still a long way off.[180] Meanwhile, the challenge is to present as wide an array of methods as possible to potential clients (the so-called cafeteria approach), so that they may select the method with the fewest "disadvantages" from their own perspective. For example, some women actually welcome the amenorrhea that accompanies the use of Depo-Provera, whereas in other countries, regular menstrual bleeding is valued as a sign of female health and future fecundity. Many users of the IUD like the fact that there is "nothing to remember" and the method does not interrupt the act of intercourse, whereas other women will not accept having a "foreign object" in their bodies. Sterilization has given a definitive solution to the contraceptive needs of women (and to a lesser degree, men) in countries around the world. Yet in many African countries, fertility potential is equated with life itself, and to voluntarily close off this vital function is unthinkable (even for those who claim to have all the children they want). In sum, one person's advantage is another person's objection. This is true not only across countries but also within a given country. For this reason, programs need to make available a wide range of contraceptive options, and in general they are able to do so. In this respect, developing countries with the assistance of external donor agencies generally offer a wider range of contraceptives— and at far lower (subsidized) prices—than is available to the average woman or man in the United States.

- *Family planning should be promoted creatively and in an entertaining format through multiple channels of mass and interpersonal communication.*

Developing countries are light-years ahead of the United States in terms of their use of the media to promote social "products," among them family planning. Billboards publicize the local brand of socially marketed condoms. Radio and television minidramas play out the tragic consequences of unwanted pregnancy or HIV. Teens watch music videos urging them to delay having sex. Truck drivers have sun visors for their windshields that advertise condoms. T-shirts and baseball caps with family planning logos further desensitize the topic of contraception.

If there was ever an area where the United States could learn from the experiences of developing countries, it is in the area of promoting health interventions through communication campaigns.[181] The strategies for designing such campaigns for maximum effectiveness are now readily available, and experience in this area abounds in the developing world. The results from such efforts consistently show the increases in knowledge of the topic, attitudes toward it, and related practices.

- *Programs must be socially and culturally acceptable.*

    In their nascent phase, many family planning programs challenged local religious and social mores. Gradually, however, as more people have become aware of the advantages of family planning, use of contraception has become more socially acceptable. Programs often identify ways to structure their activities so as to conform better to community norms.[182] For example, religious leaders may be brought in to ensure their followers that family planning is an acceptable practice. Programs in Latin America often offer natural family planning (e.g., rhythm, the calendar method, Billings[183]) to Catholics who do not wish to disobey the edict from the Vatican against artificial forms of contraception. In earlier days, programs often required a husband's consent before a woman could get family planning help, to reduce fears that family planning would undermine the traditional decision-making structure in marriages. (This requirement has been dropped from most programs, as women's reproductive rights have become more salient). Instead, family planning programs succeed best when they introduce new ideas that may challenge conventional norms but do not violate the deep-seated values of the majority.

- *Programs must operate on the principle of voluntarism.*

    Curiously, the programs with the greatest impact at the population level are those that appeal to personal motives of the target population and present family planning as a desirable commodity that helps people achieve their own reproductive intentions. Thailand is the shining example of this principle.

    Despite the widespread adherence to the Buddhist faith and the traditional values held by its people, Thailand has been among the most successful countries in changing the contraceptive behavior of its population. With contraceptive prevalence at 72 percent (or 70 percent for modern methods), it has attained replacement-level fertility (TFR of 2.0). Although early campaigns alluded to the benefit of smaller families for the socioeconomic development of the country, the primary focus was on the benefits of family planning for the individual. Moreover, Thailand has been a role model for other countries in its ability to "de-medicalize" family planning and to convert this taboo concept into a household word. More than any other country, Thailand has made family planning "fun." As early as the 1980s, school children were taught the "multiple uses" of condoms, one age-appropriate activity being balloon-blowing contests. Youngsters had the opportunity to see and touch this device in a totally nonsexual context. Mass communications increased awareness of family planning and helped to reshape the cultural norms regarding family size. Again, the focus was on the benefits to the users. Contraception became widely available, not only in government clinics but from a vast network of community-based distributors—themselves trusted members of the community. Family planning was woven into the fabric of the community: the CBD worker who owned a beauty salon would give users a discount on haircuts, the CBD worker who was also an agricultural extensionist rented his ox at a discount to couples using a method. Taxi drivers in the capital city, Bangkok, carried displays of contraceptives on their dashboards and were trained to explain the products to their customers. A man in a rural area wanting a vasectomy could combine a trip to the city for that purpose with a bus tour of the city's monuments. On the king's birthday, vasectomies were free. In short, the success of the Thai program can be linked to three important characteristics:

- contraceptives were readily available at affordable prices,
- promotion of family planning was aggressive but client-centered and lighthearted,
- the spirit of voluntarism pervaded all activities.

If there is one lesson to be learned from the past 30 years, it is that the most successful family programs are those that avoid focusing on the motive of "population control" and, instead, take a client-focused approach to promoting contraceptive use. In practical terms, how can this work? We will look at this question, focusing on a number of different demographic scenarios.

CHAPTER 9

Prescription for Action for the 21st Century

What is the most rational course of action regarding population for the 21st century?

There is no blanket solution. We recognize the myriad social, cultural, political, and economic factors that affect fertility decisions in countries worldwide. Moreover, the importance placed on population as a demographic issue and on women's health as a social issue varies dramatically from one country to another. For example, Bangladesh, with its meager government resources, nonetheless finances a third of the costs of its highly active family planning program while Saudi Arabia, with a per capita income of over $10,000, has no official family planning program. It is naive to think that if we were just able to identify the right solutions, we could convert the leadership of sovereign countries around the world to act accordingly. Indeed, the organizers of the 1974 World Population Conference learned the folly of this notion.

It is important to recognize that fertility is on a downward course. The social and economic factors that influence the demand for children and in turn the demand for contraception will continue to operate in the vast majority of countries in ways that favor lower fertility. Nevertheless, there remains an urgent need to promote family planning in those countries with fledgling or stagnated programs. It is instructive to consider alternative courses of action for different demographic scenarios. To this end, we have classified some 151 countries with data available from the U.S. Bureau of the Census (comprising over 99 percent of the world's population) into categories based on two variables that affect the future growth of the countries: *current fertility* and the *severity of the AIDS epidemic*. The resulting clusters of countries suggest alternative approaches that serve both the reproductive health needs of the populations involved and the goal of curbing population growth.

Classification Scheme

The two variables used in this classification are (1) *total fertility rate* (TFR)[184] in a given country, and (2) *HIV seroprevalence rate*[185] among "low-risk," urban adult populations.

As mentioned in the early chapters of this book, both fertility and mortality define the population growth rate in the absence of migration (births minus deaths equals natural increase). Although we tend to focus on fertility as the culprit for rapid population growth, mortality plays an important role. Over the past half century, declining mortality has fueled population growth as countries have developed more effective strategies of "death control." However, we have not included mortality rates per se as a factor in the following categorization for several reasons. First, crude death rates are highly skewed by the age composition of the population and thus misleading in cross-national comparisons. For example, the crude death rate is lower in Mexico than in the United States because Mexico has a larger percentage of youth. Second, mortality rates tend to show less variation than fertility rates because effective death control techniques have been adopted worldwide. And third, current mortality rates are just beginning to reflect the impact of the AIDS epidemic—which will be felt far more in 20 years as those infected with HIV succumb to the illness. Rather, the percent seropositive for HIV more accurately measures the potential impact of the AIDS epidemic on mortality rates in the coming years.[186]

It is important to recognize that the reported levels of HIV prevalence in a given population are "best guesses," not precise measures. For financial, political, and ethical reasons, few attempts have been made to measure HIV at the national level, although a few studies have taken population-based measures of HIV among populations targeted for intervention programs.[187] Statistics on seroprevalence rates tend to come from women attending prenatal clinics or from military recruits. Although lacking precision, they are suggestive of the prevalence of HIV infection in a given area. *Low-risk population* refers to adults in the general population ages 15–49 in urban areas ("typical people"), whereas *high-risk populations* include groups such as commercial sex workers, migrant workers, truck drivers, and men who have sex with men, whose occupations or lifestyles put them at higher risk of HIV transmission. In the remainder of this chapter, the term *general population* is used to describe the low-risk population.

The classifications and the criteria for these classifications are as follows:

- High fertility, low HIV:
  - TFR: greater than or equal to 4.5 births
  - HIV seroprevalence: less than 5 percent among the general population in urban areas
- High fertility, high HIV:
  - TFR: greater than or equal to 4.5 births
  - HIV seroprevalence: 5 percent or higher among the general population in urban areas
- Diminishing fertility, low HIV:
  - TFR: 2.2–4.4 births
  - HIV seroprevalence: less than 5 percent among the general population in urban areas
- Diminishing fertility, high HIV:
  - TFR: 2.2–4.4 births
  - HIV seroprevalence: 5 percent or higher among the general population in urban areas
- Countries with replacement-level fertility or below:
  - TFR: less than or equal to 2.1 births
  - HIV seroprevalence: measured or presumed to be less than 5 percent

For developing countries, the Bureau of the Census is the primary source of HIV prevalence data. This information tends to be most complete for urban areas, and thus classification of countries by HIV status in this chapter is based on this urban low-risk adult population aged 15–49. The Bureau of the Census incorporates mortality due to HIV into its population projections once a country has an HIV prevalence of at least 5 percent in urban areas. No HIV prevalence data were available from Somalia and Sierra Leone, and thus these two countries have been excluded from the analysis in this chapter.

By contrast, for Western Europe and the rest of the industrialized world, the most complete source of HIV prevalence data is UNAIDS. However, this latter source reports data for the low-risk adult population in urban and rural areas combined. UNAIDS incorporates mortality due to HIV into its population projections once a country reaches 2 percent prevalence in the combined urban and rural (i.e., total national) population. Thus, the two data sources are not, strictly speaking, comparable (and in a very limited number of cases— Mozambique and Benin—they disagree). For the purposes of analysis in this chapter, this is not a problem, since no industrialized countries have HIV levels of 5 percent or higher among the urban low-risk adult population.

Distribution of Countries by Classification

HIGH FERTILITY, LOW HIV

One-fifth of the countries in the world (31 of 151) fall in this category as shown in figure 9.1. Since countries vary dramatically in size, it is also useful to assess the percent of the world's population that corresponds to this scenario: 8 percent as shown in figure 9.2. This set of 31 countries demonstrates the population dynamics common to almost all developing countries in the post–World War II period: high fertility coupled with decreasing mortality, resulting in rapid population growth (see table 9.1). These countries, beset by economic crisis and (in some cases) political unrest, have one advantage over their counterparts in scenario 2 (below). As yet, HIV levels have remained relatively low.

Half of these countries (16 of 31) are in sub-Saharan Africa. They are characterized by low levels of socioeconomic development: per

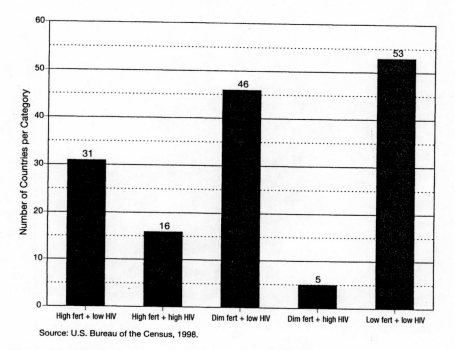

Source: U.S. Bureau of the Census, 1998.

Figure 9.1—Distribution of Countries: Fertility and HIV Status

capita income averages just over $300 per year. Women continue to have an average of at least six births for the multiple and complex reasons discussed in chapter 7.

The group also includes a handful of Asian countries with sustained high fertility: Bhutan, Cambodia, Laos, Nepal, and Pakistan. They share certain characteristics with their African counterparts: low levels of socioeconomic development, a recent history of civil unrest, and/or little political will to promote family planning.

The only Latin American country with sustained high fertility is Guatemala. Although fertility has declined among the Spanish-speaking majority (to a TFR of 4.3 in 1995), the high fertility norm persists among the 40–50 percent of the population that is Mayan (whose TFR is 6.8).[188] Interestingly, the conditions for sustained high fertility found for Africa and Asia apply to this Mayan population: low levels of living, a recent history of civil unrest, and a government openly hostile to family planning.

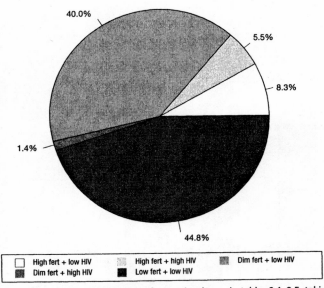

Note: This chart is based on the distribution of countries shown in tables 9.1–9.5, taking into account the actual size of the population in each country.

Source of data: U.S. Bureau of the Census, 1998.

Figure 9.2—Percent of World Population by Category

In addition to the 22 countries for which we have TFR and HIV data, there are 9 countries—largely from the Arab world—that have high fertility and very low levels of HIV. In the oil-rich countries of the Arab world, high fertility is maintained by strongly pronatalist norms and a lack of economic pressure at the family level that has caused fertility to decrease elsewhere. In other countries, low levels of living (resulting in low education, high infant mortality, and other unfavorable social conditions) and lack of political will explain the persistent levels of high fertility.

Although the countries in this category have low levels of HIV prevalence, this is no reason for complacency. In contrast to fertility rates that change only gradually, HIV levels can escalate quickly, as the case of Botswana illustrates. One of the most promising African countries in the 1980s with impressive economic growth, rational management of natural resources, and strong governance, Botswana is currently struggling with an AIDS epidemic that seems to have struck

REGION	TOTAL FERTILITY RATE	HIV PREVALENCE IN GENERAL POPULATION/URBAN AREAS ONLY	HIV PREVALENCE IN GENERAL POPULATION/URBAN AND RURAL AREAS
Sub-Saharan Africa			
Angola	6.2	1.2	2.1
Benin	6.5	1.0	2.1
Chad	5.7	4.1	2.7
Congo (Kinsasa)	6.5	4.3	4.4
Eritrea	6.0	3.0	3.2
Gambia, The	5.9	0.6	2.2
Guinea	5.6	0.7	2.1
Guinea-Bissau	5.2	2.6	2.3
Liberia	6.1	4.0	3.7
Madagascar	5.8	0.1	0.1
Mali	7.0	4.4	1.7
Mauritania	6.4	0.5	0.5
Mozambique	6.0	2.7	14.2
Niger	7.3	1.3	1.5
Senegal	6.2	1.7	1.8
Asia			
Bhutan	5.2	0	0
Cambodia	5.8	3.2	2.4
Laos	5.7	0.8	0
Nepal	4.9	0	0.2
Pakistan	4.9	0.6	0.1
Afghanistan	6.0	missing	0
Latin America			
Guatemala	4.8	0.4	0.5
North Africa and Middle East			
Iraq	5.2	missing	0
Jordan	4.8	missing	0
Libya	3.9	missing	0.1
Oman	6.1	missing	0.1
Saudi Arabia	6.4	missing	0
Sudan	5.7	3.0	1.0
Syria	5.6	missing	0
West Bank	4.9	missing	missing
Yemen	7.1	missing	0

Table 9.1—Group #1: Countries with High Fertility and Low HIV Prevalence

Note: In the countries shown above with no HIV data available for urban areas only (labeled "missing"), it is presumed to be <5%. In the HIV data for urban and rural areas, the West Bank's prevalence rate is included in Israel's.

Source of data for TFR and HIV rates (urban only): U.S. Bureau of the Census, 1998. Source of data for HIV rates (urban and rural): UNAIDS, 1998.

overnight. In the capital city of Gabarone, HIV prevalence among pregnant women skyrocketed from 8 percent in 1990 to 34 percent in 1997. In addition, HIV prevalence is reported to have reached 43 percent among pregnant women in Francistown (1997).[189] Among the group of countries listed in table 9.1, four (Chad, Democratic Republic of the Congo,[190] Liberia, and Mali) already have HIV prevalence levels of 4.0 or above among the general population in urban areas.

HIGH FERTILITY, HIGH HIV

Sixteen of the 151 countries fall into this category, and they represent about 6 percent of the world's population (see figure 9.2). The population dynamics in these 16 countries are similar to those in the first group: high fertility coupled with declining mortality in recent decades resulting in rapid population growth. This group of countries, all located in sub-Saharan Africa except Haiti, include many of the nations hardest hit by the AIDS epidemic.

As shown in table 9.2, the percent of the general population in urban areas infected with HIV ranges from about 6 to 34 percent. In Malawi and Rwanda, one-third of adults in urban areas are HIV-positive. Particularly tragic, many of these countries had made significant gains in increasing life expectancy in recent decades. But the AIDS epidemic has reversed that trend. Ten years ago, life expectancy at birth was 48 years in Rwanda. In the absence of AIDS it would have been 54 by now; instead it is currently 42 years. Similarly, life expectancy in Malawi has been reduced by 15 years due to AIDS.[191]

Fertility has undergone little change in these countries; the TFR averages six children per woman in this group. However, in a number of the countries afflicted by AIDS, it is now clear that mortality rates will rise dramatically, decreasing population growth (as yet, not to the point of zero or negative growth). For example, in Malawi the rates of natural increase are expected to drop from 1.7 percent in 1998 to 0.7 percent in 2010. A similar drop from 2.5 percent to 1.2 percent is expected in Tanzania. If the rate of new infections declines by 2010, the population growth would again begin its upward trend based on high levels of fertility. By contrast, if the epidemic continues to esca-

REGION	TOTAL FER-TILITY RATE	HIV PREVALENCE IN GENERAL POPULA-TION/URBAN AREAS ONLY	HIV PREVALENCE IN GENERAL POPULA-TION/URBAN AND RURAL AREAS
Sub-Saharan Africa			
Burkina Faso	6.6	12.0	7.2
Burundi	6.4	23.2	8.3
Cameroon	5.9	5.7	4.9
Central African Republic	5.1	9.3	10.8
Congo (Brazzaville)	5.0	7.1	7.8
Cote d'Ivoire	6.0	12.5	10.1
Ethiopia	6.9	17.5	9.3
Malawi	5.6	34.0	14.9
Namibia	5.0	17.6	19.9
Nigeria	6.1	6.7	4.1
Rwanda	5.9	32.7	12.8
Tanzania	5.5	13.7	9.4
Togo	6.6	16.5	8.5
Uganda	7.1	15.3	9.5
Zambia	6.4	27.3	19.1
Latin America			
Haiti	4.7	8.4	5.2

Table 9.2—Group #2: Countries with High Fertility and High HIV Prevalence
Source of data for TFR and HIV rates (urban only): U.S. Bureau of the Census, 1998.
Source of data for HIV rates (urban and rural): UNAIDS, 1998.

late, zero or negative growth could occur in selected countries (see figure 9.3).

DIMINISHING FERTILITY, LOW HIV

This category contains a sizeable number of countries: 46 of the 151 total (30 with HIV data, another 16 with missing data but HIV levels presumed to be less than 5 percent) (see table 9.3). Together, this group of countries represents 40 percent of the world's population. Fertility levels have at least begun to drop, and in many cases they have dropped to near replacement-level fertility. Nonetheless, almost all of the countries in this group continue to experience population growth due to high fertility levels in the past. Moreover, they have experienced

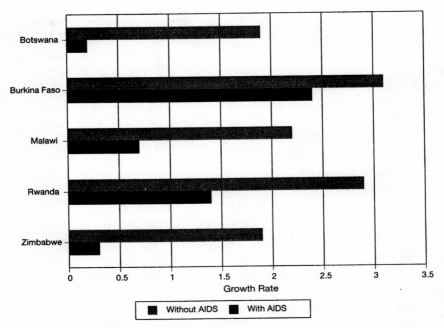

Growth Rate

Without AIDS   With AIDS

Source: U.S. Bureau of the Census, 1998.

Figure 9.3—Growth Rates with and without AIDS, Selected African Countries, 2010

relatively low levels of HIV prevalence. This group of countries includes several distinguishable clusters, as follows:

Family planning success stories. It is difficult to quantify the extent to which fertility decline is the result of family planning programs or improved social and economic conditions. In some cases, the effects of family planning predominates, whereas in many others, socioeconomic development is more important.[192] This being said, many of the countries in this category have had very active family planning programs, including Bangladesh, Colombia, Dominican Republic, Egypt, El Salvador, India,[193] Indonesia, Jamaica, Mexico, Peru, Tunisia, and Vietnam.[194]

Favorable socioeconomic conditions. High levels of education for females and strong economic conditions tend to reduce the demand for children, and a solid public/private health infrastructure makes services available to different levels of society. These factors help to

REGION	TOTAL FER- TILITY RATE	HIV PREVALENCE IN GENERAL POPULA- TION/URBAN AREAS ONLY	HIV PREVALENCE IN GENERAL POPULA- TION/URBAN & RURAL AREAS
Sub-Saharan Africa			
Gabon	3.8	4.2	4.3
Ghana	4.3	3.6	2.4
Mauritius	2.2	missing	0.1
Asia			
Bangladesh	3.0	0	0
Burma/Myanmar	3.7	1.3	1.8
India	3.2	2.5	0.8
Indonesia	2.6	0	0.1
Malaysia	3.4	0	0.6
Mongolia	2.8	0	0
Papua New Guinea	4.3	0.2	0.2
Phillipines	3.5	0	0.1
Vietnam	2.5	0.3	0.2
Latin America			
Argentina	2.7	2.8	0.7
Brazil	2.3	2.7	1.0
Chile	2.3	0.1	0.2
Colombia	2.9	1.1	0.4
Costa Rica	2.8	0	0.6
Dominican Republic	3.1	2.0	1.9
Ecuador	2.8	0.3	0.3
El Salvador	3.1	0.5	0.6
Honduras	4.1	4.1	1.5
Jamaica	2.3	2.0	1.0
Mexico	2.9	0.6	0.4
Panama	2.6	0.8	0.6
Uruguay	2.3	0.1	0.3
Venezuela	2.7	0.1	0.7
Bolivia	4.1	missing	0.1
Nicaragua	4.3	missing	0.2
Paraguay	4.3	missing	0.1
Peru	3.3	missing	0.6
North Africa and Middle			
Egypt	3.4	0	0
Iran	2.6	0	0
Morocco	3.4	0.2	0
Tunisia	2.4	0	0
Turkey	2.5	0	0
Algeria	3.4	missing	0.1
Israel	2.7	missing	0.1
Kuwait	3.4	missing	0.1
Lebanon	2.3	missing	0.1
United Arab Emirates	3.6	missing	0.2

continued on next page

Table 9.3—Group #3: Countries with Diminishing Fertility and Low HIV Prevalence

In the countries shown above with no HIV data available for urban areas only (labeled "missing"), it is presumed to be <5%.

Source of data for TFR and HIV rates (urban only): U.S. Bureau of the Census, 1998.
Source of data for HIV rates (urban and rural): UNAIDS, 1998.

REGION	TOTAL FER-TILITY RATE	HIV PREVALENCE IN GENERAL POPULA-TION/URBAN AREAS ONLY	HIV PREVALENCE IN GENERAL POPULA-TION/URBAN & RURAL AREAS
Europe			
Albania	2.6	missing	0
Azerbaijan	2.7	missing	0
Kyrgyzstan	2.7	missing	0
Tajikistan	3.5	missing	0
Turkmenistan	3.3	missing	0
Uzbekistan	2.9	missing	0

Table 9.3—Group #3: Countries with Diminishing Fertility and Low HIV Prevalence (continued)

explain the presence of Argentina, Chile, Uruguay, and Venezuela on this list, despite the Catholic heritage of these countries.

Widespread abortion. In countries of eastern Europe and the former Soviet Union, fertility levels historically have been lower than in the countries of the developing world. For some women, abortion serves as their main method of family planning in the absence of other forms of contraception.[195]

DIMINISHING FERTILITY, HIGH HIV

This group of five sub-Saharan countries—Botswana, Kenya, Lesotho, South Africa, and Zimbabwe—includes the most successful family planning programs in sub-Saharan Africa. Although fertility has yet to approach replacement level in any of these countries (TFRs range from 3.2 to 4.1), they represent the beginning of a demographic transition toward lower fertility in Africa.[196] However, their "success" is overshadowed by the specter of high levels of HIV (see table 9.4). It is indeed a cruel fate that the countries that have pioneered the promotion of smaller families—Zimbabwe, Botswana, and Kenya in particular—now must contend with AIDS.

Because of population momentum, there is usually a lag of 40–50 years between the period when a population achieves replacement-level fertility and zero population growth. Ironically, the two African countries most successful in lowering birth rates through family planning—Zimbabwe and Botswana—are expected to "achieve" a popula-

REGION	TOTAL FER-TILITY RATE	HIV PREVALENCE IN GENERAL POPULA-TION/URBAN AREAS ONLY	HIV PREVALENCE IN GENERAL POPULA-TION/URBAN AND RURAL AREAS
Sub-Saharan Africa			
Botswana	4.0	42.9	25.1
Kenya	4.1	24.6	11.6
Lesotho	4.1	31.1	8.4
South Africa	3.2	15.8	12.9
Zimbabwe	3.9	32.0	25.8

Table 9.4—Group #4: Countries with Diminishing Fertility and High HIV Prevalence

Source of data for TFR and HIV rates (urban only): U.S. Bureau of the Census, 1998.
Source of data for HIV rates (urban and rural): UNAIDS, 1998.

tion growth rate of 0.2–0.3 percent in the span of a generation (by 2010) (see figure 9.3). In 2015, Botswana's population will be 20 percent smaller than it would have been in the absence of AIDS.[197] Had AIDS not been a contributing factor, the population community would have lauded the accomplishments of these countries in lowering growth rates. However, the dramatic decline in growth rates resulting from AIDS brings a sense of defeat, not accomplishment. Even more discouraging, those who will succumb to AIDS constitute the potentially most productive citizens: adults of reproductive age.

COUNTRIES WITH REPLACEMENT-LEVEL FERTILITY OR BELOW

Among countries that have reached replacement-level fertility, HIV prevalence is not a key consideration for population growth for two reasons. First, fertility rates are already low. Second, the countries in this category that do have data on HIV prevalence are believed to have low rates among the general population in urban areas. For example, Thailand—widely cited as a country with an AIDS problem that it has effectively addressed—has an HIV prevalence of 2.1 percent among the general population in urban areas. All other countries that have measured HIV report 1 percent or less prevalence among the general population in urban areas. In short, AIDS remains a public health problem of enormous proportions, but it is not a factor in population growth in countries with low fertility. Thus, in this part of the analysis we discuss all countries with replacement-level fertility or below, irrespective of the availability of HIV data (although those without HIV data are listed as such in table 9.5).

This group of 53 countries includes several distinguishable clusters, as follows:

- *Industrialized regions:* North America, Western Europe, and other industrialized nations (Australia, New Zealand, Japan).

- *Recently developed (or still developing) countries with strong family planning programs, in some cases coupled with improved socioeconomic conditions:* China, Cuba, Singapore, South Korea, Sri Lanka, Thailand.

- *Nations of the former Soviet Union and Eastern Europe:* Countries with historically lower fertility and/or widespread abortion such as Moldova, Ukraine, and Georgia.[198]

- *Others:* Demographic "outliers" including Puerto Rico (which is an anomaly because of its relationship to the United States) and North Korea.

Promoting Contraceptive Use under Seven Distinct Scenarios

The classification of countries by TFR and HIV status yields one category with replacement-level fertility or below (group #5) and four categories of countries with fertility above replacement level (groups #1–4). Further discussion of the countries with below replacement-level fertility is presented in chapters 10 and 11. The remainder of this chapter is devoted to the four categories with fertility above replacement level, characterized by

- High fertility, low HIV
- High fertility, high HIV
- Diminishing fertility, low HIV
- Diminishing fertility, high HIV

Within the four categories are clusters of countries that differ markedly in terms of the factors influencing their population dynamics and the approaches needed to address population growth. Thus, in the final section of this chapter, we expand these four categories to

REGION	TOTAL FER-TILITY RATE	HIV PREVALENCE IN GENERAL POPULA-TION/URBAN AREAS ONLY	HIV PREVALENCE IN GENERAL POPULA-TION/URBAN AND RURAL AREAS
Asia			
China	1.8	0.0	0.1
Hong Kong SAR	1.4	0.0	0.1
Japan	1.5	0.0	0
Singapore	1.5	0.0	0.2
South Korea	1.8	0.8	0
Sri Lanka	2.1	0.0	0.1
Taiwan	1.8	0.0	missing
Thailand	1.8	2.1	2.2
Australia	1.8	missing	0.1
New Zealand	1.9	missing	0.1
North Korea	1.6	missing	0
Latin America			
Cuba	1.6	0	0
Trinidad and Tobago	2.1	1.0	1.0
Puerto Rico	2.0	missing	missing
North America and Europe			
Armenia	1.7	missing	0
Austria	1.4	missing	0.2
Belarus	1.3	missing	0.2
Belgium	1.5	missing	0.1
Bosnia/Herzegovina	1.1	missing	0
Bulgaria	1.1	missing	0
Canada	1.7	missing	0.3
Croatia	1.5	missing	0
Czech Republic	1.2	missing	0
Denmark	1.7	missing	0.1
Estonia	1.3	missing	0
Finland	1.7	missing	0
France	1.6	missing	0.4
Georgia	1.5	missing	0
Germany	1.3	missing	0.1
Greece	1.3	missing	0.1
Hungary	1.5	missing	0
Ireland	1.8	missing	0.1
Italy	1.2	missing	0.3
Kazakhstan	2.1	missing	0
Latvia	1.2	missing	0
Lithuania	1.5	missing	0
Macedonia	2.1	missing	0
Moldova	1.9	missing	0.1

continued on next page

Table 9.5—Group #5: Countries with Replacement-Level Fertility or Below

Note: In the countries shown above with no HIV data available for urban areas only (labeled "missing"), it is presumed to be <5%. In the HIV data for urban and rural areas, Taiwan's prevalence rate is included in China's, and Puerto Rico's rate is included in the United States'.

Source of data for TFR and HIV rates (urban only): U.S. Bureau of the Census, 1998. Source of data for HIV rates (urban and rural): UNAIDS, 1998.

REGION	TOTAL FER-TILITY RATE	HIV PREVALENCE IN GENERAL POPULA-TION/URBAN AREAS ONLY	HIV PREVALENCE IN GENERAL POPULA-TION/URBAN AND RURAL AREAS
Netherlands	1.5	missing	0.2
Norway	1.8	missing	0.1
Poland	1.4	missing	0.1
Portugal	1.4	missing	0.7
Romania	1.2	missing	0
Russia	1.3	missing	0.1
Serbia	1.8	missing	missing
Slovakia	1.3	missing	0
Slovenia	1.2	missing	0
Spain	1.2	missing	0.6
Sweden	1.8	missing	0.1
Switzerland	1.5	missing	0.3
Ukraine	1.4	missing	0.4
United Kingdom	1.7	missing	0.1
United States	2.1	missing	0.8

Table 9.5—Group #5: Countries with Replacement-Level Fertility or Below (continued)

seven scenarios requiring different approaches to promoting greater contraceptive use while addressing the HIV/AIDS problem, recognizing that any program must be tailored to the political realities and cultural idiosyncrasies of the country in question. These seven scenarios include the following:

- High fertility, low HIV:
  - in sub-Saharan Africa and Asia (1)
  - in the Arab countries of the Middle East (2)
- High fertility, high HIV
  - in sub-Saharan Africa (3)
- Diminishing fertility, high HIV
  - in sub-Saharan Africa (4)
- Diminishing fertility, low HIV
  - with strong family planning programs (5)
  - with favorable economic conditions (6)
  - with historically lower fertility and/or widespread abortion (7)

Common to the prescription for all seven scenarios are the ingredients for desirable and effective family planning (described in chapter 8): strong political commitment and program leadership, widespread access to contraception through multiple mechanisms, adequate choice of contraceptive method, client-oriented quality services, widespread promotion through mass and interpersonal channels, socially and culturally acceptable approaches, and voluntarism. However, in the remainder of this chapter we outline particular areas of focus consistent with the conditions present in each scenario.

SCENARIO #1: HIGH FERTILITY, LOW HIV IN SUB-SAHARAN AFRICA AND ASIA

Countries in this category share four characteristics: inadequate health care infrastructure including for family planning, lack of political will for family planning, ineffective management of existing resources, and high infant mortality related to extreme poverty. The challenges under these circumstances seem almost insurmountable. Yet these are the countries with the greatest need for action. What can be done?

Link family planning to efforts to ensure child survival. Before they can afford to have fewer children, couples must have assurance that their offspring will live to adulthood. In the context of Africa, integrated services (family planning with maternal/child health and, to an increasing extent, AIDS prevention) are the norm. The promotion of birth spacing generally results in lower fertility, but it is also an important step to ensure the survival of the youngest child.[199] Indeed, the birth spacing message has been well received in countries where the survival of children is precarious, precisely because it speaks to a primary concern of parents.

Enlist greater participation of nongovernmental organizations (NGOs). Many donors have become frustrated with governmental development programs for a variety of reasons: their unwillingness to take a stand on politically sensitive issues, lack of priority placed on family planning and reproductive health, lack of adequate human resources to carry out the technical aspects of the work, and mismanagement of funds, to name a few. As a result, many donors are moving toward greater support of the NGO community.

Make quality family planning services more readily available. This is not a new idea; indeed, it is the current mantra for most development agencies, including USAID with its MAQ (Maximizing Access and Quality)Initiative. However, it remains the sine qua non for increasing family planning. Local governments and NGOs with assistance from donor agencies must ensure a constant supply of contraception to developing countries. They must find means of delivering services to all parts of the country, including rural areas, in culturally appropriate ways. Moreover, they must develop an approach to service delivery that now characterizes successful programs: treating clients with dignity, listening to their needs, satisfying those needs with minimal bureaucratic hassle and inconvenience, and in the process creating a positive image for family planning. This remains one of the greatest challenges, precisely because of the constant attention that it requires.

Create greater social acceptance of smaller families. Because of persisting high fertility, large families remain the norm. With urbanization, exposure to mass media, and access to contraception, there will be a natural tendency toward a gradual reduction in fertility. In situations where social norms continue to support large families, the mass media can play an important role in reminding couples of the alternatives that exist to continued childbearing and the multiple benefits from family planning.

SCENARIO #2: HIGH FERTILITY, LOW HIV IN THE ARAB COUNTRIES OF THE MIDDLE EAST

The Arab world demonstrates the same extremes in the acceptance of contraception as mentioned at the beginning of chapter 7 for the major regions of the developing world.[200] On the high end is Iran, reporting a surprisingly high contraceptive prevalence of 73 percent. There is also a cluster of countries in the 50–60 percent range that have actively pursed family planning over a sustained period and are now seeing results. Tunisia, a pioneer in family planning, has one of the highest levels of prevalence in the region (60 percent). Morocco has made excellent progress (contraceptive prevalence rate [CPR]=50 percent) despite lower levels of female education and more socially conservative norms. Jordan is another country in the region that has attained midlevel prevalence (CPR=53 percent). These countries know how to promote family planning; Tunisia has even "graduated" from receiving international assistance from certain donors given its level of technical capacity and development. They will continue to benefit from continued international backing of their programs, as the low fertility norm takes hold in these midrange countries.

The oil-rich countries have a fairly low prevalence—for example, United Arab Emirates (28 percent), Kuwait (35 percent), Oman (24 percent), and Qatar (36 percent). These statistics reflect the strong cultural norms for large families combined with higher per capita income (and generous government services) to support additional children. They also represent an important deviation from the pattern found elsewhere in the world that a high standard of living translates into low fertility. However, it is important to note that several of these countries' governments feel population growth is too low, despite the fact that their annual population growth rates are among the highest in the world.[201] These countries remain outside the sphere of influence of the international population community because its high per capita income excludes them from international funding and their desire to maintain their strong cultural identity precludes their looking to the West for better means of promoting family planning.

Yemen has made the least progress in family planning (7 percent prevalence), consistent with the high infant mortality rates, low levels of education, and weak health infrastructure in that country. In this sense, it conforms to the profile and prescription of scenario #1.

SCENARIO #3: HIGH FERTILITY, HIGH HIV IN SUB-SAHARAN AFRICA

These countries represent the greatest challenge to the population/ public health community because they must simultaneously confront the AIDS epidemic while promoting the relatively unpopular practice of family planning. Their family planning infrastructure is uniformly lacking: all countries in this category were classified as "weak" or "very weak/none" on an internationally recognized Family Planning Program Effort Index, which measures political support, service and service-related activities, recordkeeping/evaluation, and availability and accessibility of contraceptive supplies and services.[202] Added to this is the burden of combating AIDS.

After considerable debate in the 1980s over the advisability of integrating family planning and STD/HIV prevention services, a general consensus now exists among the public health community regarding this marriage. Whatever the debate on its pros and cons (outlined in chapter 8), service integration is increasingly common in African countries with high levels of HIV infection. In this context, it is important to consider three subgroups within the general population whose needs must be addressed.

First are *HIV-infected individuals,* though the vast majority do not know their sero-status and seemingly would prefer not to. Staff available at integrated service facilities must be able to discuss the pros and cons of becoming pregnant with technically accurate information (e.g., probability of the child's being infected, effect of pregnancy on the mother's health) and extreme sensitivity to the situation. Westerners might dismiss pregnancy under such conditions as irresponsible, but the question must be considered in light of the extreme social pressures to produce offspring in most African cultures. Anecdotal evidence exists to suggest that some young women may try to speed up the childbearing process, precisely to ensure having children before they become afflicted with the virus.

Second, clinic personnel must help *women who are at substantial risk of infection*—those in a "monogamous relationship" with a spouse who is not. This situation is also extremely sensitive, since condom use within marriage is highly unpopular in most of Africa. A woman may hesitate even bringing up the topic for fear that her husband or partner will suspect *her* of infidelity or, worse yet, become violent because of the discussion. To further complicate matters, the woman may not know the exact extent of her partner's infidelities, making it hard to judge how important condom use might be to her own health and survival. Efforts are under way in most high-HIV-prevalence African countries to train service providers in counseling techniques that include HIV/AIDS prevention, but the challenge of reaching the millions who would benefit from counseling is daunting.

Third, services must address the needs of *women who are seemingly at low risk of AIDS and also want to control their own fertility,* as do their counterparts throughout the world. Ironically, we used to think of this task as being supremely difficult in the context of strongly pronatalist African cultures. Yet with the additional challenge of AIDS, the family planning component begins to look like the easy part, especially as economic pressures and urbanization make large families less feasible.

To summarize, for the countries in this category, an essential part of their strategy must be to integrate STD/HIV/AIDS prevention with family planning for humanitarian and public health (not demographic) reasons. However, the countries in this group share much with those in Scenario #1, the difference being in the level of HIV prevalence. Thus, several of the points mentioned under the first scenario are equally applicable here:

- Link family planning to efforts to ensure child survival.

- Enlist greater participation of NGOs.

- Make quality family planning services more readily available.

SCENARIO #4: DIMINISHING FERTILITY, HIGH HIV IN SUB-SAHARAN AFRICA

This group of five countries includes those considered most successful in introducing family planning in the context of pronatalist sub-Saharan Africa. Four of the five—Botswana, Kenya, South Africa, and Zimbabwe—have been rated as "moderate" to "strong" on the Family Planning Program Effort Index.[203] Moreover, the levels of living in several of these countries are much higher than the average for sub-Saharan Africa, a factor that favors both sustained program interventions and acceptance on the part of target populations.

The main theme of this book is the importance of curbing population growth. Yet in this set of five African countries, the programmatic focus should combine concern over rapid population growth with concern for combating AIDS. Family planning services should concentrate on (1) expanding the reach of family planning services and (2) using the family planning service delivery network to help combat AIDS. Integrated services (discussed under scenario #3 above) are the cornerstone to this strategy. Similarly, services must deal with the subgroups outlined earlier: women infected with HIV, married women at risk because of their husbands' extramarital activities, and the typical family planning client (married women at low or unknown risk of AIDS).

However, in this scenario two additional groups warrant special attention: (1) unmarried youth (who worldwide tend to fall outside the net of conventional family planning services), and (2) women whose precarious economic situations lead them into risky sexual practices for survival reasons.

Because of the success of family planning programs in these countries, the use of contraception is more widely accepted than in most other African countries. Having achieved this first step, programs are more willing to move beyond the conventional target group (married women with children) to others recognized to need their services. Just as these countries were pioneers in family planning, so they have taken a lead in adolescent programs, Kenya and South Africa in particular. As the effects of AIDS become more severe (with the escalating number of infected persons dying, leaving spouses and family members to cope), an increasing number of women of reproductive age will find themselves fending for their own survival and that of their children. Many will have no alternative but to exchange sexual favors for cash or other monetary gifts. Programs must branch out beyond clinics into the communities to reach these women.

Donor agencies like winners. Not surprisingly, they have actively supported this group of countries in their efforts to promote family planning over the past two to three decades, with the exception of South Africa, which came back into the fold only after President Mandela assumed power. These countries have demonstrated their effectiveness in promoting contraceptive use, albeit after many years of effort. The donors need to assume that these nations will be equally effective in implementing programs to combat AIDS, and they need to commit themselves—as they did for family planning—to the long run.

SCENARIO #5: DIMINISHING FERTILITY (FROM STRONG FAMILY PLANNING), LOW HIV

In these countries, the contraceptive revolution is in full force, whether the result of dedicated leadership, innovative programming, steadily improved economic conditions, or a combination of the three. These are the countries that have scored high on the Family Planning

Program Effort Index. They have demonstrated their ability to implement effective programs; smaller families have become a societal norm. Despite their successes, they continue to be faced with three challenges: serving an increasing numbers of clients, improving the quality of services, and funding the cost.

The absolute number of persons entering the 15-to-19-year range (thus beginning their reproductive period) is on the rise in almost every developing country in the world. Thus, existing services would need to expand, even if the demand for services were constant. Yet in these countries that have successfully promoted family planning, the demand for contraception continues to increase. Two factors fuel the potential demand for services in the future: more people in the age range and a greater percentage of these interested in using such services. Moreover, in many of the "successful" countries, programs are moving beyond the delivery of services to the conventional target population of married women to include unmarried adolescents. This need seems particularly urgent where the risk of unwanted pregnancy is coupled with the risk of STD/HIV infection.

A second major concern in mature programs is to improve the quality of services. Countries that have reached a minimal level of coverage in terms of contraceptive availability are working to make services more client-friendly. The Bruce/Jain framework on the elements of quality of care has served to guide the efforts of programs around the world in improving their performance in terms of the choice of methods, information given to the client, provider-client interaction, technical competence of service providers, mechanisms for ensuring follow-up, and a wider range of services available at a given facility.[204]

Finally, a major concern for these countries is not only how to achieve a high prevalence of contraceptive use but how to continue to pay for it.[205] In many countries, contraceptives are given away free of charge or at highly subsidized prices at government facilities. However, this does not represent a sustainable strategy in the long term.[206] Many of the affiliates of the International Planned Parenthood Federation, especially in Latin America, are struggling to gain greater financial self-sufficiency, which in some cases has meant a shift from a "social focus" (giving services and products away free of charge for the benefit of the low-income population) to a more commercial focus where payment of services is required. Another example comes from Indonesia, where a major objective of the national family planning program has been to convert users from the public to the private sector. Other countries are experimenting with new approaches to cost recovery, such as the sale of noncontraceptive products at a profit to subsidize the sale of contraceptives to low-income clients. Sustainability has become the buzzword, and it is not likely to go out of fashion since donors are increasingly disinclined to fund these "graduate" countries. The search continues for ways to survive on their own.

SCENARIO #6: DIMINISHING FERTILITY (FROM FAVORABLE SOCIOECONOMIC CONDITIONS), LOW HIV

This set of countries is rarely discussed in terms of successful family planning for two reasons. First, a large part of their "success" is due to the socioeconomic conditions that bring about lower fertility by placing a premium on the "quality" of children. Because of their economic means, couples can often afford to seek out the necessary services in the private sector, much as is the case with middle- and upper-class Americans. In this case, lower fertility can occur in the absence of a program per se. Second, we tend to know less about these programs because they are not recipients of donor assistance, including technical assistance requiring in-country visits. As such, they are not subject to the same scrutiny by international donor agencies and their technical partners anxious to see how well population programs are faring in different countries.

What "strategy" is needed in these countries? None that is not already in operation. These countries have achieved lower fertility thanks to favorable economic conditions that reduce the demand for children and provide citizens with the means to act on their fertility desires. They have achieved these results with little interference from the larger donor community and can reasonably be expected to follow a similar path in the future.

SCENARIO #7: DIMINISHING FERTILITY (FROM WIDESPREAD ABORTION), LOW HIV

Countries that present the anomalous picture of relatively low fertility (TFR less than 2.0) and low levels of contraceptive use raise the strong possibility of widespread use of abortion. For example, Moldova has a TFR of 1.9 and a CPR of 22 percent; the Ukraine has a TFR of 1.4 and a CPR of 23 percent. In this case, there is an obvious motivation for controlling fertility at the individual level, suggesting that access (physical and/or economic) to family planning services may be inadequate. In the post-Cairo era, it is essential that programs improve the range of services available to women, such that they are able to control their fertility without resorting to the harmful practices of abortion or becoming infertile due to untreated sexually transmitted diseases. Information and education about methods need to be strengthened since there are widespread misconceptions about contraception. Postabortion family planning services are particularly appropriate in this environment but, to date, have been far less available than what is required.

To conclude, many readers familiar with the widespread adoption of the Cairo agenda—toward a more expansive set of reproductive health services and away from a narrow focus on family planning—may wonder why the authors have chosen to "revert back" to a strong emphasis on family planning and to single it out for special attention. Indeed, there is global consensus on the Cairo agenda: almost all of the 180 nations attending the ICPD endorsed the Programme of Action, which called for a change in the focus of population policy and for commitment of resources to meet previously neglected health needs. Why not just get on the bandwagon?[207]

We recognize the many positive benefits that are expected to result from the expansion and reform of health services to better meet the reproductive health needs of women and men worldwide. We heartily applaud the efforts to improve women's status and increase gender equity as a basic human right. These are indeed goals that every government should strive to attain, and the Cairo conference was revolutionary in directing the attention of the world community to these previously neglected (or at least underfunded) areas.

What remains troublesome about the Cairo agenda was the deliberate effort to focus attention away from the goal of curbing rapid population growth. Yes, increased gender equity and women's empowerment are expected to result in lower fertility. Yet the treatment of the subject at Cairo sent the message that curbing population growth is no longer a legitimate goal to pursue. It is possible that technological solutions will be developed to increase the food supply to feed the future generations, to reforest the planet, to dissipate pollution, to improve living conditions in the burgeoning squatter communities around the world. Yet what if they don't? We fail to see how others can dismiss the issue of continued population growth as yesterday's problem.

PART III

Response to Potential Population Decline

CHAPTER 10

Population
Decline

After centuries of continuous population growth throughout most of the world, most people consider it to be a "fact of life." Very simply, "populations grow." The consequences, sometimes long term, are seldom considered even by those who should know better.

Not only is population growth a given, but most college programs in economics herald such growth and its "economic" advantages. Of course, little or nothing is said about the negative consequences of overpopulation on resources, the environment, and the quality of life. Perhaps it is time to offer courses in "The Advantages of Population *Decline.*"

The very use of that expression brings fear into the minds of most people. To borrow from the title of the excellent book by Teitelbaum and Winter, there is a "fear of population decline."[208] Our discussion of such a demographic drop in certain countries is not new. As we will see, it has been discussed with some trepidation, off and on, for many years, if not centuries.

However, before examining the details of what population decline really means, it might be advisable to look briefly at some demographic terms and concepts to better understand just where we are going—or not going—in the 21st century. First and foremost, throughout this book, we do not make demographic predictions. Rather, these are demographic *projections.* We make certain assumptions about present and future levels of fertility, mortality, and migration and, based on these assumptions, develop future projected populations. If the mathematics are correct, the projections are also correct. However, the assumptions may well be wrong—and regrettably, they are often so. Our projections, generally taken from the United Nations and from our own calculations, are simply models that indicate what a population (and its composition) will be *if* certain levels and trends of the three demographic variables (*fertility, migration, mortality*) are followed. To put it another way, if we continue our current demographic behavior, this is what will happen in the 21st century. But, as we know from past experience, changes do occur in our demographic behavior, especially in fertility.

Fertility

Fertility is difficult to measure accurately as it is subject to rapid change. As demographers, we are expected to have a quick and definitive reply to the question, How many children are women having nowadays? Yet it is technically impossible to do so. The simplest measure is the *crude rate:* the number of births divided by the total midyear population of a given year. However, the denominator may be misleading. Are there more men or women? Is this an old or a young population? Obviously, a city like St. Petersburg, Florida, with a huge retired population will have a very low crude birth rate because very few births occur in this "seniors" community. That is one reason for calling the rate "crude."[209] But this is not the reply to the aforementioned query. The *total fertility rate* is usually the measure relied on to give the best answer. This is the result of a sum of the age-specific fertility rates of a given year. It tells us the number of births women would have *if* they maintained those rates throughout their reproductive years—which seldom happens. A better measure, in one way, is the number of children ever born to women age 40 or 45 and over. That is *completed fertility.* But it hardly addresses the question of "nowadays." Thus we rely on the total fertility rate, knowing full well that it could vary from year to year. In looking at the projections in this book, one should always bear in mind that they are models and that the real world usually varies somewhat from those models. In other words, they tell you what the population would be *under specific conditions.*

Despite rapid growth of world population over the past few centuries, we must recall that for most of human history, growth was very slow. Indeed, on numerous occasions (e.g., during the Black Plague in Europe in the 13th century) population fell, sometimes quite rapidly. Thus, maintaining and even increasing population size was a natural impulse among humans for centuries upon centuries. We need only recall the Biblical maxim "Be fruitful and multiply"—appropriate advice when it was given, when the population was probably less than 1 billion. It was accepted by humans—and unfortunately still is by many, even as we approach 6 billion inhabitants on this planet.[210]

Teitelbaum and Winter explain it well:

> Discussions of population decline have almost always conjured up a multitude of alarming images. Many of them have revealed fears not only about numbers but also about the quality, vitality, or optimistic outlook of a nation's inhabitants. The interchangeable and overlapping nature of quantitative and qualitative statements inevitably adds elements of confusion and emotion to many reflections on this subject. In some cases there is clearly a presumption that the phenomenon of "decline" leads naturally to "fall."[211]

In this century, France has perhaps been the leading "worrier" about population decline. Much of the blame for the loss in the Franco-Prussian War in the late 19th century has been attributed to the difference in the populations of Germany and France. Since then, the country has been consumed with the need to have more than "fifty million Frenchmen." This emphasis on growth has been especially true of many politicians, of both the Left and the Right. For example, political leader and now president Jacques Chirac was quoted as early as 1984 as stating:

> Two dangers stalk French society: social democratization and a demographic slump. . . . If you look at Europe and then at other continents, the comparison is terrifying. In demographic terms, Europe is vanishing. Twenty or so years from now, our countries will be empty, and no matter what our technological strength, we shall be incapable of putting it to use.[212]

While Chirac may have spoken like a typical politician, he may have proved to be a fairly good prophet, although Europe is far from empty. By 2000, France's population will still not have reached the 60 million mark.

Another form of fear of population decline was noted in England at the beginning of the 20th century. While pronatalism was strong, it did not approach that of France. However, class differences were noted, especially as a result of the poor performance of "lower class" recruits in the Boer War in South Africa. The story has been repeated many times: the rich have few children; the poor have far too many. Thus, while Britain's population was not falling, the "quality" was shifting, and this too was a major concern for the political leadership of the country. Such thinking gave birth to the questionable "science" of eugenics.

One of the results of this "problem" was the enacting of legislation mandating medical inspection and improved feeding of school children. In addition, health officers were instructed to pay more attention to children's health problems, especially in poor districts. But the overall purpose was to make certain that a sufficient number of young men reached adult age so as not to endanger the population size of the potential "military" group. Thus, the fear of population decline was not limited to sheer numbers; age composition and social status were also considered seriously.

World War II contributed even more to the "problem" of underpopulation and population decline. While the Allied forces were victorious over Germany, France did fall to its archenemy in 1940—and to a considerable extent, this loss was blamed on demographic problems. Citing once again from Teitelbaum and Winter, Robert Debre and well-known demographer Alfred Sauvy wrote in 1946:

> The terrible failure of 1940, more moral than material, must be linked in part to this dangerous sclerosis [resulting from low birth rates]. We saw all too often, during the occupation, old men leaning wearily towards the servile solution, at the time that the young were taking part in the national impulse towards independence and liberty. This crucial effect of our senility, is it not a grave warning?[213]

In Britain, there was continuous worry over a declining group (the British) holding onto its far-flung empire, comprised primarily of people of other races. British medical officer Arthur Newsholme perhaps expressed it best:

> It cannot be regarded as a matter of indifference whether the unfilled portions of the world shall be peopled by Eastern races (Chinese, Japanese, Hindus etc.), by Negroes, by Slavonic or other Eastern European peoples, by the Latin races, or by the races of Eastern Europe. . . . Every Briton will wish that his race may have a predominant share in shaping the future destinies of mankind.[214]

A similar line of thinking came out of Eastern Europe when a Swiss economist wrote in 1934, "we must take note of the risk of another great invasion westward by the peoples of the East whose inferior living conditions would impel them westward."[215]

Thus, without further comments from other scholars of the day, some of whom were actually eugenicists, it is clear that prior to the enormous population growth that followed World War II throughout the world, genuine concern was being expressed not only about population decline itself but, as the eugenicists argued, about the "quality" of that population.

While the term *demographic suicide* may not have been used during this period, it is nevertheless an appropriate expression of what was occurring (and may be occurring today in certain countries). A country cannot exhibit below-replacement fertility for very long without noting increasingly rapid declines in fertility. In an earlier chapter we cited the example of Germany; however, the example is applicable to any country that exhibits for a considerable length of time a fertility rate that is below replacement.

Admittedly, demographic suicide cannot be allowed to occur. While a falling population is undoubtedly beneficial to the entire planet if attributable to low fertility, there is a lower limit, as we have already discussed. Fertility levels slightly below replacement (about 1.7 to 2.0) should be encouraged. However, when they fall to around 1.5 or lower (as in certain European countries today), the long-run possibilities of too-rapid population decline must be considered.

Do not be mistaken: a decline in population size, especially through lowered fertility, is a positive development for all of humankind. Demographer Lincoln Day says it best:

... a lot can happen before these populations [i.e. those with very low fertility] experience numerical declines to any arguably serious extent; and secondly, that to wring one's hands over present demographic trends in these countries is not only to commit the error of misplaced emphasis but to risk the enactment of irrelevant or undesirable social policies, as well. The concern over these trends appears to be based less on an awareness of their likely consequences than on the fact of moving on to unfamiliar demographic ground before social attitudes and institutions are quite ready for it.

... These countries still have more to lose socially and environmentally from past *increases* in population size, and *unevenness in age structures* in consequences of past fluctuations in birth rates, than they do from any near-zero population growth rates or the transition to persistently older age structures.[216]

As we have seen, low fertility is not a new phenomenon, especially in advanced countries. As recently as the 1930s, low fertility was a cause of concern in many countries. However, today's fertility is even lower than in the 1930s (at least in some countries), and the current low fertility is of much longer duration than it was in that decade. Indeed, there is little evidence that it will climb much in the near future. Thus, there remains the possibility that reverse momentum could lead to large population losses.

Nevertheless, rather than expressing concern about population decline (or more specifically falling fertility), we should be pleased with current developments and hope that they continue for some time to come. In discussing possible "optimum populations," demographer Lincoln Day reminds us that no population can increase indefinitely. Population growth must end—at some point.

There are limits: to resources, to physical space, to social space ... there will be a point—even with the most judicious use of the environment and the most prudent pattern of human behavior—beyond which increases in population will inevitably result in declines in the quality of life. In fact, in consequence of the existence of limits, one could argue that a truly optimum population would have a *negative*, not a zero, growth rate; a negative rate so that human numbers—however efficient the use made of the environment—would be regularly brought into line with a steadily decreasing quantity of resources. Certainly, the current period of growth in the world—both economic and demographic—can be little more than a tiny interlude in human history.[217]

The bottom line is this: some population decline is fine; low fertility is even better; but beware of extremes. The power of the momentum—whether positive or negative—is awesome and must always be considered a possibility.

The challenge for those countries where fertility has already fallen to dangerous levels—such as Italy (1.2) and Germany (1.3)—is this: How can fertility in such countries be increased *slightly*—so slightly that it would not contribute to any world population growth? We should add that by *slightly*, we are referring to increases in the total fertility rate of 0.1 or perhaps as high as 0.3. Such relatively minor increases can contribute considerably to eliminating potentially dangerous gains in population—a problem much worse than population decline, as Lincoln Day has stated (see n. 24). Total fertility rates in the vicinity of 1.7 to 2.0 would be quite appropriate and would still be below replacement.

It is difficult to imagine a total fertility rate lower than Italy's 1.2. Thus, it seems reasonable to assume that some increases will occur in the near future without any "outside" encouragement. This has already happened in the Scandinavian countries where fertility, though still slightly below replacement, has risen considerably since Sweden became the first country to register a rate under 1.5. Indeed, the Swedish system of offering additional advantages for women to become employed and remain employed even after their first birth is a model that should be followed by other low fertility countries. Even in the United States the rate has increased ever so slightly from 1.7 to about 2.0 in recent years. However, we remind the reader to review our earlier discussion of the meaning of total fertility rate.

As we reach the millennium, it appears that fertility levels in the advanced nations of Europe, as well as in Japan and the advanced "descendant countries" of British origin, will remain quite low. Some increase may occur, but it would be surprising if any country reached replacement fertility (about 2.1) in the next few years. On the other hand, any continuation of very low fertility (1.2 to 1.5) lasting a few decades would be cause for alarm. Clearly some slight increase is necessary.

Migration

Should fertility levels fall so low that population decline becomes an almost permanent problem, one "solution" is to increase immigration from other countries. Such a solution is appealing to some. One reason is that the number, rate, age, and even composition of the group of newcomers can be regulated—at least in theory. We emphasize "in theory" because that seldom turns out to be the case. Immigrant families plead their cases for allowing relatives to migrate also. Some may be well trained; many others are not. One perceived advantage is that if they are trained for the jobs for which workers are in short supply in the receiving country, they are an immediate source of labor. This all seems good but isn't really an advantage in numerous instances. *Are* the immigrants adequately trained? Another question that can be especially important is, What about communications (language)? There are also serious potential cultural issues, which are addressed below.

If a country is forced to rely on immigration to maintain what is considered to be a large enough population, it must also realize that immigrants generally have larger families than do the native-born residents, especially if the host country is advanced (which is usually the case). The contribution of immigration to population growth therefore might be much greater than originally anticipated. Combined with the fact that the host population's fertility is very low (and presumably will remain low), we have the makings of an entirely "new" society. This scenario has occurred in places such as Belize, where through immigration and higher fertility, Hispanics have replaced the Belizean descendants of English traders as the dominant population.

Immigration may be a temporary solution to declining population (if decline is viewed as a problem by the host country). However, it is far from being *the* solution. Even if the newcomers are deliberately selected for their youth and talents, they too will soon grow old, adding thousands or millions to the already swelling numbers of elderly in these counties. So while such movements may appear to be a simple answer to the problem of declining population, many other factors must be considered and will be discussed later in this chapter.

Mortality

Earlier, we somewhat facetiously remarked that raising mortality is definitely not a humane—or moral—method of lowering rapidly growing populations. Indeed, everything should be done to increase life expectancy and health everywhere. Now let's turn the tables.

In part I of this book, we noted that many millions of Americans are in today's population as a result of mortality declining since the beginning of this century. To be blunt, they simply didn't die (or their parents didn't die), making it possible for them to have children later in life. Admittedly, mortality rates—whether measured by life expectancy or death rates—are already considerably lower in most European countries than in the United States and elsewhere. The same is true of infant mortality. Yet much could be done to lower them even more everywhere.

We are only beginning to discover some of the "life savers" originating from our biodiversity and our medical laboratories. It seems that almost every day, a new discovery is announced that will improve our health and, eventually, lead to longer lives. More and more, scientists are talking about living much longer lives.

The life expectancy in Japan is over 80 years at birth and is approaching that in Sweden, while in Russia it is but 70 and in Portugal, 75. Similarly, only four infants (under age 1) are expected to die per 1,000 births in Japan, but in Italy and the United States, almost twice as many are expected to die (infant mortality rates). Clearly, there is still considerable room for improvement in increasing life expectancy (and, in the process, lowering death rates) in almost every advanced country in the world. Such success would be extremely helpful in minimizing the population decline now attributable to very low fertility.

Initially, reduction in population size is viewed as a good trend. As the rate falls even more and lasts for one or more decades, however, concern is expressed over what to do about it. Such a problem is not new, and it is with us today, especially in many European countries and Japan. Again we ask, What do we do about it? At first, we should rejoice.

Fewer people are a distinct advantage—less crowding, fewer problems in finding classrooms, and so on. Later, we begin expressing some concern as we note that neighboring countries, usually to the south, are not losing but rather gaining population, and quite rapidly. Will we be swallowed up by them? In the preceding pages, we have offered suggestions as to how to end *rapid* population decline. Fertility can be raised a bit—it doesn't take much of an increase when you consider that in the United States, a boost from 1.9 to 2.8 would result in a net growth of over 100 million people in about 60 years.[218]

Immigration is always a ready (but dangerous) answer to the problem of perceived underpopulation. Billions of humans desire to come to the United States. Numerically, that too is a "solution." Probably the best approach is to continue our recent success in curing killer diseases and thereby lowering the death rate. Perhaps the answer lies in all three factors—slightly increasing fertility, admitting a specified number of selected immigrants, and increasing life expectancy.

At any rate, all countries (including the United States) should set population policies as to the maximum number of inhabitants who can benefit from a decent quality of life. As noted scientist Edward O. Wilson recently wrote:

> The time has come to speak more openly of a population policy. By this I mean not just capping the growth when the population hits the wall, as in India and China, but a policy based on a rational solution of this problem: what, in the judgment of its informed citizenry, is the optimal population. . . . The goal of an optimal population will require addressing, for the first time, the full range of processes that lock together the economy and the environment, the national interest and the global commons, the welfare of the present generation with that of future generations. The matter should be aired not only in think tanks but in public debate.[219]

Composition of the Population

AGE COMPOSITION

Two secondary but equally important problems evolve out of tinkering with fertility, mortality, and migration: *age* and *ethnic composition.* Most countries experiencing very low fertility usually have high life expectancy; that is typical of advanced countries and results in an "old" population. In Norway, for example, 19 percent of the population is under 15, and 16 percent are 65 or over. On the other hand, Chad's population under 15 is 44 percent, while only 3 percent are 65 or over.[220] Caring for an old population (i.e., with perhaps 15 to 20 percent of the population over age 65) is an expensive proposition. Raising fertility will lower the median age a bit, but the elderly are still there and increasing in number. Relying on immigration is a losing strategy—immigrants get old too! And it goes without saying that increasing life expectancy in an advanced country usually means that the old live longer—resulting in more elderly than originally projected.

An older population is more "expensive" than a younger population. One example is the cost of hospitalization. According to a study in Australia, assigning 100 as a constant for ages 35–49, the hospitalization rate (as a percentage of 100) for males 75 and over was 457 and 222 for females. The average length of stay in a hospital was 285 for males and 385 for females, compared to 100 for the group aged 35–49.[221] Similar examples are numerous. In the United States we are currently in the midst of a heated debate as to how to take care of the elderly that will emerge from the baby boom sometime after 2010.

A rapid shift in any of the demographic variables is bound to play havoc with the age composition of the nation. The huge baby boom that has "haunted" the United States since the late 1940s remains with us and will for some time to come, culminating in the forthcoming "senior boom." Furthermore, the baby boom itself has an "echo." Although baby boom young women have fewer children than their parents, they are so numerous that even with lowered fertility, the *number* of births is climbing. At this writing in the late 1990s, over 4 million births occur every year, a number as high as in the peak years of the original baby boom. Thus, the impact of that giant generation will be felt—though less and less over time—perhaps for another century. Age composition will fluctuate; we simply must adapt to such fluctuations. More important, we should prepare ourselves for the next fluctuation in age composition. That is the only way we can address large and rapid shifts in fertility.

Shifts in mortality, though not as dramatic, also can be a tremendous problem. Many European countries suddenly found themselves with a shortage of male adults as a result of World War II. This shortage contributed to the need to accept more immigrants in economically growing countries such as Germany and France. Immigration, unless it is monitored very closely, can affect the age composition of a nation. In the United States we talk about the enormity of the baby boom, but we neglect to add that during the same period, immigration was reaching highs approaching those noted at the turn of the 20th century. Many of those newcomers were of "baby boom" age; many were born here and became "baby boomers" of a different nationality.

To reiterate, any sudden shift, whether in fertility, mortality, or immigration, will have serious impacts on the age composition of a nation. An old population has very different problems than does a young population.[222]

ETHNIC COMPOSITION

Immigration by itself presents several serious problems to both the host and sending countries. We have alluded above to the matter of cultural adaptation and the accompanying problem of language difficulties. Some countries, such as the United States and Canada, have a long history of accepting immigrants from sources all over the globe. Canada admittedly has had a historical bicultural problem concerning Quebec and the other nine provinces. Nonetheless, in both countries (and elsewhere), new immigrants—and more so, their children and grandchildren—adapted quite well in the past. Looking primarily at the United States, we can take pride in the fact that one does not have to be of Anglo-Saxon background to succeed whether culturally, economically, or politically. Perhaps the best example was noted in 1980 when Michael Dukakis, a second-generation American of Greek origin, ran for president on a major ticket. But much earlier, in 1960, both major political parties offered American voters the choice for vice president of two second-generation Americans: Spiro Agnew (of Greek origin) and Edmund Muskie (of Polish descent). The United States has passed the era when even being a Catholic was a barrier to running for high public office.

Whether or not we like it, being white remains a decidedly positive factor in advancing in one's chosen job or profession. But even in this area, we are beginning to see some progress (although not fast enough).

What is an American? That question really has no answer; or rather, the answer keeps changing over time. We are always redefining "American" as new groups immigrate to this country. Thus far, the process of cultural adaptation has been quite successful among non-Hispanic whites. But we have a long way to go in accepting the minorities that will, by the middle of the 21st century, comprise together a majority of the population. That is to say, among non-Hispanic whites, African Americans, Asians and Pacific Islanders, and Hispanics, no one group will represent over 50 percent of the population. The United States will be the first truly universal nation. That is a challenge that some European countries may have to face if they accept numerous immigrants (such as Turks in Germany and Algerians in France). A new kind of adaptation will have to occur in countries unaccustomed to such a process.

The United States is probably the best example of a fairly successful program of cultural adaptation where groups of different backgrounds—whether race, ethnicity, or religion—manage to meld into a single group (or approximately so). Whenever a country such as Germany, for example, is suddenly saddled with a large non-German population, some type of cultural adaptation must occur. At one extreme, the two groups could deliberately remain separate from each other (a benign form of apartheid). This mode of adaptation could be called *cultural separatism.* Newcomers are socially isolated from the resident group either through their own volition or through segregationist practices by the host group. The slave-freeman relationship exemplifies cultural separatism, as does that between the dominant American society and religious groups such as the Amish. At the other extreme is what might be called *cultural amalgamation,* where a new society and culture results from widespread intermarriage between the two groups. The racial blending in 19th century Latin America that led to the emergence of mestizos is an example of cultural amalgamation.

Between these extremes are pluralism, assimilation, and the so-called melting pot. In pluralism (sometimes called multiculturalism), the society allows its constituent ethnic groups to develop, with each emphasizing its particular cultural heritage. Such a mode of adaptation is encouraged in Canada. Assimilation assumes that the new groups will take on the culture and values of the host society and gradually discard their own heritage. Following the seminal study by sociologist Milton Gordon, cultural assimilation (or acculturation), where a subordinate group takes on many of the characteristics of the dominant group, is distinguished from structural assimilation, where that subordinate group gains access to the principal institutions of society but maintains its own culture.[223]

In the melting pot—primarily an American concept—the host and the immigrant groups share each other's cultures, and in the process a new group emerges. Consequently, the melting pot differs somewhat from pure assimilation, although some scholars treat them almost synonymously. While early advocates of the melting pot theory encouraged newcomers to assimilate into American society, the society they envisaged was not intended to be totally dominated by Anglo-Saxons. Rather, it was a new society formed by the blending of the various white groups, albeit with strong Anglo-Saxon influence. Whether the melting pot has worked remains debatable. We would argue that—although it took longer than anticipated—it did work, but only for the non-Hispanic white population. The examples cited earlier, and many others, are testimony to the success of a "white melting pot" in the United States.

It hasn't been easy for the people of the United States to adjust to the changes caused by ethnic variation. Throughout American history, immigrants as well as residents have had to adapt to each other; a process of cultural adaptation was necessary if the society was to survive. A brief examination of the U.S. situation may serve as a potential model for other countries that may become more heterogeneous through increased immigration.

Even before America's independence in 1776, ethnic groups already maintained separate cultures and languages. Benjamin Franklin, for one, was concerned lest Pennsylvania become "Germanized." "This Pennsylvania will in a few years become a German colony; instead of their learning our language, we must learn theirs, or live in a foreign country."[224] Franklin was exaggerating, as the new nation remained solidly Anglo-Saxon even with the presence of numerous minorities. But despite the Anglo-Saxon dominance, with independence came a new feeling of nationalism. Participation in the Revolutionary War legitimized the claims of non-English Europeans to a full share in the new nation, and by 1790, the United States was truly a mosaic of peoples, though predominantly western European.

A second wave of newcomers began to arrive in the early part of the 19th century. Many were either Catholic or Jewish and came mainly from Ireland and Germany. By 1850, Catholicism was the largest Christian denomination in the land—with Catholics comprising 7.5 percent of the population. In many large cities, Catholics were rapidly becoming the majority. It was during this period that native-born Americans began to display ambivalent feelings about immigration.

Cultural adaptation was not as simple a process after 1840 as it had been earlier, when the non-English European groups had assimilated into the Anglo-American population. After 1840, different types of immigrants entered the country. Catholics and Jews threatened the Protestant domination of the country; Asians and Mexicans entered (or were annexed) in what some considered to be alarming numbers. These two groups (as well as African Americans) were prohibited from entering the mainstream of American culture—a clear example of cultural separatism.

By the 1880s, while Anglo-Saxons remained solidly in economic power, new immigrant groups worshiped differently and in some cases were of different racial backgrounds than earlier groups. The ethnic mosaic was becoming more diverse.

After 1880, a "third wave" of immigrants arrived. The majority came from eastern and southern Europe and most were either Catholic or Jewish; many were poor and illiterate, even in their own language. While the movement of African Americans out of the south into the north was not across national boundaries, it had many of the same characteristics of international migration and helps elucidate the increasing heterogeneity in northern cities around the turn of the century. Together, these diverse streams contributed to the creation of yet another image of America. It also called for a new mode of cultural adaptation. The ethnic mosaic was changing more rapidly than ever.

At the beginning of the 20th century, the Anglo-American majority favored the total assimilation of new European groups into an

Anglo-dominated society. (It was taken for granted that Mexicans, Asians, and African Americans would remain culturally separate.) Cultural pluralism and even the melting pot were adamantly opposed. Theodore Roosevelt felt nothing but disdain for "hyphenated" Americans, and Woodrow Wilson declared that "Any man who thinks himself as belonging to a particular national group in America has not yet become an American."[225]

A "fourth wave" began after World War II and was composed primarily of Hispanics and Asians. Because of changes in immigration legislation, the doors were literally opened for millions of newcomers from Latin America and Asia. Today, about three-quarters of all immigrants come from these two regions, almost the opposite of a few decades ago when about three-quarters came from Europe. And once again, the immigration issue is being debated. For our purposes, the answer to, What is an American? is changing. Not only are most immigrants now coming from Asia and Latin America, they come from just about all of the countries on these two continents. Thus, school classrooms with 50 to 60 different countries represented are no longer the exception in some of the nation's larger cities where immigrants are numerous.

As we look back over the past century to assess how the cultural adaptation process among persons of European ancestry developed, it is clear that pressures to "Americanize" everyone through total assimilation were not entirely successful. Most European groups retained some semblance of ethnicity over the years while at the same time adapting to new surroundings. Neither has cultural pluralism been particularly successful among European immigrants and their descendants. In recent decades, serious attempts have been made to revive some form of ethnic pride. If cultural pluralism means that various groups maintain cultural and structural separatism from each other—thereby creating the possibility of also maintaining cultural patterns different from those of the "host" society—then the evidence suggests that this form of cultural adaptation has not succeeded among most Americans of European ancestry.

By the 1980s and early 1990s, the melting pot had worked quite well for immigrants and their descendants from southern and eastern Europe, structurally as well as culturally. But the melting pot may be working in a different way than had been anticipated. In addition to different groups acting increasingly alike, a new population is form-ing—the unhyphenated Americans.[226] In addition, the power elite, historically almost exclusively white Anglo-Saxon Protestant, is being replaced by one in which persons of non-WASP heritage are commonplace.[227]

It has taken some two or three generations for the melting pot to "come to a boil." But by the mid–20th century, major changes began to occur. We have already cited the changes in the political spectrum. But in business, a second-generation Italian American, Lee Iacocca, reached the top. In higher education, the late A. Bartlett Giamatti served as president of Yale University and later as commissioner of major league baseball. John Lombardi is president of the University of Florida. Former senator George Mitchell as well as John Sununu, adviser to former President Ronald Reagan, are both of Arabic extrac-tion. The change has been gradual and subtle, but a glance at any daily newspaper reveals that a person's ethnic and religious background (as opposed to race) are hardly ever mentioned.

Can the relative success achieved in the adaptation of the third-wave immigrants and their descendants into a new kind of America be duplicated with the fourth wave, with its mix of racially diverse groups and with African Americans still waiting in the wings to be part of the mainstream? The question of how the United States is to maintain a unified country out of peoples from all over the world is one that can-not be ignored for long.

It seems unlikely that a repetition of the successful melting pot process will occur, given the situation in 2000 as compared to that in 1980. The differences in economic structure, in the possibilities of interethnic marriages, in the increasing emphasis on group rights, and particularly in the level of immigration are far too great to envision a new interracial melting pot in the foreseeable future. What then are the alternatives?

We hope cultural separatism is a thing of the past. Yet there are those who would favor such a process. A few Hispanic irredentists dream of a new Spanish-speaking southwest as a way to take back demographically what the United States took militarily some 150 years ago. And there are a few segregationists who would dearly love to keep all the races separate and "in their places." Sad to say, the last two decades have witnessed a growth in the intensity of such bigoted behavior. Writing in 1987, author Kurt Vonnegut expressed it beautifully:

> The darkest secret of this country, I am afraid, is that too many of its citizens imagine that they belong to a much higher civilization somewhere else. That higher civilization doesn't have to be another country. It can be the past instead—the United States as it was before it was spoiled by immigrants and the enfranchisement of Blacks.[228]

Neither is the total cultural assimilation of the new minority groups (i.e., the complete surrender of immigrants' symbols and values and their absorption of the core culture) a realistic goal. Soon there may be no majority in which to assimilate. In fact, the English are no longer the numerical majority of all non-Hispanic whites in the United States. Furthermore, there is considerable doubt as to whether the current majority or the newer groups desire total assimilation. The choices lie between cultural pluralism (or multiculturalism) and a new mode of adaptation we have labeled pluralistic assimilation. (This concept will be discussed later in more detail.) Whatever direction the nation follows will determine the kind of United States that will evolve in the 21st century.

A benign form of cultural pluralism has long been a part of American life. Ethnic enclaves are still present in large cities. Diverse religious and cultural holidays remain on the calendars of many Americans. However, beginning in the 1960s, cultural pluralism took on a different meaning. European ethnic groups began to clamor for "rights" similar to those bestowed on African Americans. To some people, "cultural pluralism implies the conscious pursuit of a national order in which Americans find their identity primarily as members of ethnic and/or religious blocs and only secondarily as individuals engaged in carving out a position in the general society."[229]

A harder-edged version of cultural pluralism is currently in vogue. The focus is on a contention that the United States is a compact between what some are beginning to lump together as a "Euro-American" population and a limited set of minority groups made up principally of African Americans, Native Americans, Asians, and Hispanics.[230]

Too often, Americans confuse the fact that they are a pluralistic nation with acceptance of cultural pluralism. America is pluralistic in the sense that many religions and ethnic groups are represented in its population and that number continues to grow. Nevertheless, it has constantly striven to achieve overall unity in its basic interests and ideals. *E pluribus unum* succinctly describes the "ideal" American nation. If cultural pluralism was but a supplement to these common interests and ideals, it would be totally appropriate. However, cultural pluralism as currently conceived is presented as an argument for the primacy of the homeland language and culture. Indeed, as the late Theodore White commented: "Some Hispanics have . . . made a demand never voiced by immigrants before. That the United States, in effect, officially recognize itself as a bicultural, bilingual nation."[231] Such cultural pluralism is not the most attractive direction for the nation to follow as it strives for more unity rather than disunity.

Pluralistic Assimilation[232]

The challenge to America, or to any country facing similar racial/ethnic problems, is to find a way to assure that all its residents, of whatever background, have equal access to all avenues to success and, in the process, adapt to American culture while contributing to its ever-changing content. At the same time, all its residents, of whatever background, must have the choice of maintaining their own subcultures within the broader American society. As the nation gradually becomes more multiracial, it is particularly important that a form of cultural adaptation be accepted that takes the best of cultural pluralism and assimilation while at the same time maintaining the American culture and assuring its acceptance by all.

Pluralistic assimilation might be appropriate if the goal of the society is to be united insofar as possible given the population's composition. All groups are assimilated, both culturally and structurally, into the already diverse mainstream society. Indeed, this is actually "assimilation among" rather than "assimilation into" and reflects the changing demographic picture and the fact that in the future, no one ethnic group will predominate. The inclusion of structural assimilation suggests that all groups will have equal access to power, whether economic, social, or political. Pluralistic assimilation, on the other hand, reflects the fact that the society is no longer composed of varying ethnic groups of the same race. Multiracial groups may maintain their identities at the same time that they become "assimilated" into the mainstream society.

The success of Japanese Americans, despite the horrors of internment during the Second World War, provides us with a working model of pluralistic assimilation. While gradually becoming assimilated culturally and structurally into the mainstream society, they remain an identifiable racial group, though increasingly, interracial marriages are occurring. It would be naive to conclude, however, that prejudice against Japanese Americans is nonexistent. Pluralistic assimilation is an ongoing process, and its eventual success will require the cooperation of all groups.

Many factors must be present if this type of cultural adaptation is to succeed. First, levels of immigration must be very limited.[233] Only in this way will the newest immigrants gradually become part of the 21st century society to which they emigrated. Pluralistic assimilation is thus particularly suited for multiracial societies where no one group predominates. It differs from cultural pluralism in that allegiance is to the nation first and to the group second; it differs from cultural assimilation in that the group maintains its identity. Pluralistic assimilation also serves to provide some heterogeneity within ever-increasing societal homogeneity. As T. S. Eliot once wrote, "A people should be neither too united nor too divided if its culture is to flourish."[234]

Reducing levels of immigration is necessary, but not sufficient, if pluralistic assimilation is to succeed. Second, the society must provide the means to make economic and social advancement possible for *all* its residents. This will involve easy and inexpensive access to higher education as well as technical training. It will necessitate a revamping of the nation's educational institutions to allow for the better preparation of *all* residents for the occupations of the future—a "G.I. Bill" for the 21st century. In other words, a new kind of structural mobility must be developed that is appropriate for the economy of the 21st century. Should these plans fail and minorities find themselves overwhelmingly in lower paying jobs while the majority is predominantly in higher paying positions, conflict will be inevitable and pluralistic assimilation will fail.

Third, future immigrants must demonstrate a strong desire to join their new neighbors and become "one of us," changing the meaning of "us" in the process. Just as most early 20th-century immigrants wanted to become American, so too should those of the early 21st century. The U.S. motto *E pluribus unum* (out of many, one) is appropriate for all nations that will face the challenges discussed above. If a nation is to accept "out of many, one," there can be no room for cultural separatism or for irredentist movements on the part of the newcomers.

Fourth, as the dominant majority loses its numerical advantage, intermarriage between ethnic and racial groups will become more commonplace. Rather than look upon such marriages with disdain, as is done by far too many people today, mixed marriages should be encouraged, as this contributes to the true formation of a real nationality. Already interracial marriages in the United States are increasing at a rapid rate. From 310,000 such marriages in 1970, the number rose to almost 1.5 million in 1990. We can only hope for a continuation of that trend.

Fifth, all forms of discrimination must end. This will be an enormous challenge in some areas. The United States remains a racist society, and that must change if pluralistic assimilation is to succeed. If it is truly desired as the mode of adaptation for the future, long-time residents must cease thinking of the newcomers as "inferior" foreigners. These motivated individuals are not the "mob at the gates." Indeed, every effort should be made to assist the newest residents to participate fully and equally in the dynamic societies of the 21st century.

Schools at all levels should develop programs to better understand the multilingual and multicultural backgrounds of all its residents, new and old. While the major groups will remain identifiable, all residents, irrespective of race or ethnicity or religion, must learn to respect **and appreciate one another simply as fellow residents. Responsibilities must be balanced with rights. John F. Kennedy's inspired words from** his 1961 inaugural address, "Ask not what your country can do for you, ask what you can do for your country," seem to have been forgotten in the selfish decade of the 1990s. For pluralistic assimilation to succeed, a stronger national community must emerge and the nation-state, be it Germany, Japan, or the United States, must do everything to ensure its continued unity through emphasis on a common language and patriotism.

"Pluralistic assimilation," "forms of interaction," "cultural assimilation," "the melting pot theory," "cultural amalgamation," and "group integration" are all examples of jargon perhaps endearing to some sociologists. But basically, these terms re-emphasize the fact that whenever one person or group moves into an area inhabited by another person or group, both must adapt to a newly defined situation.

In this chapter, we have concentrated on the pattern of adaptation in the United States because it has perhaps had more experience than any other nation in receiving newcomers by the millions. As many other nations—especially those with very low fertility—turn to immigration as a possible solution to their demographic problems, the experience of the United States may be of some use to them as they try to maintain their identity, language, and culture.

Germany, for example, has a growing number of non-Germans living there permanently. By now there are third-generation Turks in Germany. The same applies to other non-German ethnic groups. These people are never considered to be "German" despite the number of generations involved. This suggests potential adaptation problems as the population of "true Germans" continues to decline and that of "non-Germans" grows. What method of cultural adaptation will Germany follow? A similar though not as extreme case applies to France and its Algerian minority.

Table 10.1 contains population projections—based on the most recent UN data—for Japan and the Philippines to illustrate the broader situation in the first half of the 21st century. Although Japan is extremely reluctant to accept immigrants, what will it do to solve its problems as its numbers diminish (if they do)? On the other hand, the Philippines, next-door neighbors almost, is growing rapidly at 2.1 percent per year (its population is now about 75 million). This comparison illustrates a potential situation between these two nations in the 21st century *if* current demographic patterns don't change.

We assume that Japan's total fertility rate of 1.43 will remain constant. For the Philippines, we assume that it will fall gradually from 3.44 in 2000 to 2.60 in 2050. The resulting differences are enormous. The

CHARACTERISTIC	JAPAN		PHILIPPINES	
	2000	2050	2000	2050
Population (000s)	126,633	122,352	75,293	155,905
Percent 0-4	4.9	3.4	13.2	8.6
Percent 5-14	10.1	7.7	23.7	16.5
Percent 15-24	12.8	8.7	19.8	15.4
Percent 65 and over	16.6	34.6	3.6	11.1
Median Age	40.8	52.7	21.4	31.9
Growth Rate	0.09	-0.9	1.93	1.16
Crude Birth Rate	10	6.7	29.1	18.1
Crude Death Rate	9.1	15.7	5.8	6.5
Total Fertility Rate	1.43	1.43	3.44	2.6

Table 10.1—Projected Population of Japan and the Philippines, 2000-2050

Philippines' population will surpass that of Japan by 2030. In fact, Japan's population will begin to drop after 2040 and its growth rate in 2050 will be –0.9, thus assuring a continued decline in numbers. As for the Philippines, even with a falling birth rate, its 2050 population will still be growing at over 1 percent annually—a doubling in less than 70 years.

The age composition differences are also quite remarkable. Note that Japan's elderly population will climb from 16.6 to 34.6 percent over the first half of the century. By 2050, over one-third of all Japanese will be elderly. The rate will also rise in the Philippines from 3.6 to 11.1 percent. In neither case do we assume any migration, in or out. The question must then be asked, Will Japan be forced to relax its long-held anti-immigration position as it sees its population drop, especially in the working ages? Will the Philippines be in a position to support more than 30 million additional residents in just 50 years, or will emigration be its "solution"?

This comparison of neighboring island countries serves to illustrate the dilemmas that many nations will face in the next century: (1) for some less developed countries, cut back on growth through reduced fertility and/or emigration, and (2) for some advanced countries where fertility is already very low, raise fertility and lower mortality if possible or increase immigration. These may prove to be *the* dilemmas of the 21st century—depending on whether a nation's population is growing, as in most LDCs, or is not growing, as in most MDCs.

CHAPTER 11

The Stationary Population

In part I of this book, we referred briefly to the stationary population and cited Sweden as a possible "real world" example that almost typifies this "model" population. Now let us go into more detail as to what might be a demographic goal for all nations and therefore for the planet at large.

Stability and Stationarity

First, it is necessary to distinguish between two confusing terms: *stability* and *stationarity*. Unfortunately, the media often uses the term "stable" to imply a no-growth situation as in "The nation's population has stabilized." Since this book is demographic in nature, we cannot accept such a broad definition. Demographers define a

stable population as the kind of population that would result if a certain set of age- and sex-specific birth and death rates, observed for a specific year, continued indefinitely into the future. If this were so, a point in time would be reached where the age and sex composition of the population would become fixed and would no longer change. The concept "stable" refers to age and sex composition, not to size. It can grow, shrink, or remain the same size. In fact, a "stationary" population is a stable population in which the intrinsic (age-specific) birth rate is equal to the intrinsic death rate. Only in this case is the size as well as the age-sex composition of the population unchanging.

In a stable population the rate of growth never changes, the crude birth and death rates are constant, the age structure is unvarying, and the sex ratio is always the same. . . . It tells us what a *real* population would eventually look like if its age-specific birth and death rates for a given year remained unchanged indefinitely. Generally, it takes about seventy years to approach stability.[235]

Thus, a stationary population is a special kind of stable population that has the same characteristics, but in addition, the population size never changes. It is also important to point out that this model applies solely to "closed populations"—that is, migration in or out is not considered.

To be sure, a stationary (or stable) population is a demographic model. In the real world, rates seldom, if ever, remain the same for a long enough period to reach a stationary (or stable) condition. Nevertheless, in a number of instances, fertility and/or mortality rates have remained at the same level for many years and stability (if not stationarity) was almost reached. In the United States, for example, the total fertility rate remained at about 1.8 for well over a decade after the end of the baby boom. It is only in this past decade that it has risen slightly to almost 2.1. Similarly, mortality rates (or, to be more accurate, life expectancy) have remained at almost the same rate with a slight improvement noted almost every year. This situation is called "quasi-stable."

The big advantage to stable (including stationary) populations is that the age-sex composition does not change as it has so tremendously in the United States and elsewhere as a result of both a baby boom and baby bust and in some countries, such as France and Russia, because of wartime casualties. Such major oscillations play havoc with policy-making at all levels and make it difficult to plan into the future. One needs only to look at the current problems facing the U.S. social security system to see a prime example of the difficulties that emerge from such wide fluctuations in fertility.

Real-World Example of Stability

As we mentioned earlier, the real world of population seldom reflects exactly the models developed by demographers. However, some come quite close. We have examined the latest UN projections to illustrate how stability works in the real world. Table 11.1 below shows data from Denmark's projected population for 2000 to 2050 as an example of real-world "almost stability." Sweden could be used as well, but Denmark's projected population is actually a better example of stationarity than Sweden's.

Between 2000 and 2050, Denmark's population hardly will change—a very slight decrease is noted. Thus, Denmark, according to these assumptions, is at zero growth. Its sex ratio barely varies over the 50-year period. Except for the proportional growth of the elderly population, other ages under 25 remain quite stable. The increase in the elderly proportion is explained by the remnants of a short baby boom and generally higher fertility in the middle to later 1990s.

The total fertility rate is assumed to rise to 2.10 by 2020 and remain at that level to 2050; however, life expectancy is expected to rise slightly over the period. This, then, is not a pure model of stability but approximates it fairly well.

A Hypothetical Stationary Population

A real-world stationary population is even more difficult to locate than a stable population—it takes a considerable amount of time to arrive at a true stationary population. Nevertheless, it is often in the

CHARACTERISTIC	2000	2010	2020	2030	2040	2050
Population	5,274	5,314	5,320	5,316	5,274	5,234
Sex Ratio	98.3	98.9	98.6	98.3	98.1	98.4
% Age 0-4	6.4	5.8	6	6.3	6	6.2
% Age 5-14	12.2	12.6	11.5	12.3	12.5	12.1
% Age 15-24	11.5	12.1	12.5	11.4	12.4	12.6
% Age 65+	14.7	16.1	19	20.8	22.5	21.1
Growth Rate	0.12	0	0.01	-0.03	-0.08	-0.08
Crude Birth Rate	12.4	11.5	12.6	12.2	12.3	12.3
Crude Death Rate	11.6	11.5	12.4	13	13	13.1
Total Fertility Rate	1.89	2.03	2.1	2.1	2.1	2.1
Life Expectancy	76.1	77.1	78.1	78.6	79.4	80.3

Table 11.1—Projected Population of Denmark, 2000–2050 (in thousands)

best interests of policymakers and people in general to at least aim for the goal that a stationary population model can give us.

To that end we have prepared a hypothetical projection of the U.S. population with stationarity in mind. First, we must determine the replacement level of fertility—that is to say, given a specified level of mortality (as measured by life expectancy) what should the total fertility rate be? In most advanced countries, including the United States, 2.1 has become an almost "sacred" replacement-level total fertility rate. A few decades ago, it was 2.2. As mortality fell, so did the replacement level of fertility. People sometimes ask why it isn't simply 2.0. A couple has two children; isn't that replacement? The answer is that only females matter in this case and since the sex ratio at birth is about 105 males to 100 females, we must account for that. Thus, the lowest the replacement-level fertility could ever reach would be 2.05. Not all infants live to maturity, however, and that too must be taken into consideration. Therefore, 2.1 is not "sacred" after all. Indeed, it could be 5.0 or higher in a developing country if mortality was very high, especially infant mortality. In other words, it would take five births for two children to reach maturity.

In our stationary model for the United States, we have projected an overall life expectancy of 80 years at birth (actually 79.85) with women living almost 10 years longer than men (roughly 85 to 75, respectively). This is somewhat higher than the current rate of about 75 years overall, so 2.1 is not the correct replacement level of fertility. We settled for 2.07 and began with the Census Bureau's projected population for the year 2000 and carried it out for 200 years to 2200. Table 11.2 summarizes our hypothetical projection.

The growth rate reaches 0.01 percent in 2050 and stays there from then on. Thus, 2.07 is just barely above the replacement level but close enough to indicate the results of a stationary population. From 2050 to 2100, just over 1 million people would be added to the population. Especially notable is the permanency of the age composition. From 2050 on, hardly any shift is noted in age structure. Similarly, the dependency ratio stays at about 65 from then on. We can conclude that if this projection had been extended for another 100 years, the same pattern would still be present in 2300, with a very slight increase in population because the true replacement level of fertility is just below 2.07. This,

CHARACTERISTIC	2000	2025	2050	2075	2100	2150	2200
Population	274,810	309,529	312,667	313,254	313,986	315,430	316,875
Crude Birth Rate	13.3	12.5	12.6	12.6	12.6	12.6	12.6
Crude Death Rate	8.6	12.1	12.5	12.5	12.5	12.5	12.5
Growth Rate	0.48	0.04	0.01	0.01	0.01	0.01	0.01
% Age 0-14	21.4	18.9	18.7	18.7	18.7	18.7	18.7
% Age 15-64	65.9	61.4	60.3	60.4	60.4	60.4	60.4
% Age 65+	12.7	19.7	21	20.9	20.9	20.9	20.9
Dependency Ratio	51.8	63	65.2	65.5	65.6	65.6	65.6

Table 11.2—Hypothetical Stationary Population of the United States, 2000–2200 (in thousands)

then, is what a stationary population would look like. If the age-specific birth and death rates equal each other (or approximately so), in about two generations a population becomes stationary—no further growth, no further changes in age and sex composition, no changes in sex ratio—an ideal demographic situation, to say the least!

A stationary population is, by definition, a closed population. That is, immigration, in or out, is not considered. However, in recent years a few demographers have studied the possibility of including net migration within the concept of stationarity. In 1982, demographers Espenshade, Bouvier, and Arthur demonstrated mathematically that it was possible to arrive at a stationary population with immigration, providing the net reproduction rates (NRR) were below replacement and the immigration was numerically constant throughout.

We have shown that any fixed fertility and mortality schedules with an NRR below one (this is approximately equal to a TFR of 2.1), in combination with any constant annual number and age distribution of immigrants, will lead in the long run to a stationary population. The size and other characteristics of this eventual stationary population depend only upon our assumptions regarding fertility, mortality, and the age-sex composition of immigrants, and are not influenced in any way by the population we begin with.[236]

This finding has tremendous implications for population policy. If one accepts the fact that immigration levels can be controlled through legislation or just through fiat, then it is actually possible to determine how to reach a certain stationary population level.

Say, for example, as in our next hypothetical projection (see table 11.3), that the United States had a TFR of 1.9 and net immigration of 100,000. Beginning in about 75 years, stationarity would be approached. While the last part of pure stationarity takes an incredibly long period to reach, at a growth rate of –0.14 we are certainly close enough to say this is indeed a stationary population. Various combinations of below-replacement fertility and constant immigration can lead to the same eventual stationary population. The important point is that once a country (or region) has determined a goal for an end to growth, it is then possible to determine how many (if any) immigrants to accept to reach that goal, bearing in mind that it takes a considerable amount of time to actually attain the goal but a relatively brief period to come close enough to say "we have done it."

Because of its original age composition (remnants from the baby boom) and immigration, the population grows for about 25 years,

CHARACTERISTIC	2000	2025	2050	2075	2100	2125	2150	2175	2200
Population	274,810	307,576	304,601	293,951	282,552	271,807	261,811	252,537	243,929
Crude Birth Rate	12.4	11.4	11.2	11.2	11.2	11.2	11.2	11.2	11.2
Crude Death Rate	8.7	12.4	13.3	13.5	13.5	13.5	13.5	13.5	13.5
Migration Rate	0.7	0.6	0.7	0.7	0.7	0.7	0.8	0.8	0.8
Growth Rate	0.45	-0.04	-0.14	-0.16	-0.16	-0.15	-0.14	-0.14	-0.14
% Age 0-14	21.4	17.9	17.1	17.1	17.1	17.1	17.1	17.1	17.1
% Age 15-64	67	62.2	61.1	61	60.4	60.4	60.4	60.4	60.4
% Age 65+	12.6	19.9	21.8	21.9	22.5	22.5	22.5	22.5	22.4

Table 11.3—Hypothetical Population of the United States, 2000–2200 (with TFR=1.9 and net immigration 100,000) (in thousands)

though by a small amount. Then, beginning about 2030 or 2035, the death rate begins to surpass the birth rate by an amount sufficient to overcome the 100,000 immigrants entering the country. Eventually a stationary growth rate of −0.14 is attained. If we continue this projection ad infinitum, the rate would eventually reach 0, but the total population at that time would be close to what it will be in 2200—244 million, or somewhat lower than it is today. Furthermore, as with the "closed" stationary population, note that the age composition reaches a point in the relative near future where no further changes occur.

If we are willing to settle for "close enough," this is an excellent model to follow, once a population policy has been established that determines how many people a nation can support—or, more specifically, its carrying capacity. Do policymakers prefer to add more immigrants or would they like to maintain close to replacement fertility and fewer immigrants? That is a policy decision, but knowing that stationarity is possible *with* immigration makes a population policy that much less difficult to achieve.

To be sure, this remains a demographic model where time is irrelevant. Yet most of the change occurs in the early years. Thus, if we recall the "perfect is the opposite of the good" proverb and are willing to settle for the general findings of this model, its premises can be a basis for population policy. Recall, of course, that fertility must remain under replacement and immigration should approximate numerical constancy. Also important is the fact that even if immigrants have higher fertility in the first few decades, as long as they eventually approximate that of the native-born population, the model will work. It will simply take longer to achieve stationarity.

Returning to reality and the real world, pure stationary demographic behavior is hardly likely to occur for any long period of time. Yet we can remain close to its parameters by assuring that fertility remains low through various incentives and continuous media attention. We can see that mortality remains at its present level (or even falls a bit—which does not detract from the model). And most important, we can make certain that immigration remains at stated levels whatever those may be. There must also be close monitoring of the demographic variables so appropriate adjustments can be made from time to time—especially with immigration. For example, it may be necessary to lower or raise levels of immigration depending on the recent rates of fertility and/or mortality. The realistic goal is to come as close as humanly possible to the requirements of the stationary-with-immigration model.

While this may seem far-fetched, eventually it may be almost required for every country in the world to set a population goal and thus to develop some version of stationarity. The ultimate goal (or is it a dream?) is to see a stationary world population with no further growth (ideally, eventually smaller than today's 6 billion) and with no problems associated with changes in age and sex composition.

PART IV

The Demographic Challenges of the 21st Century

CHAPTER 12

What Lies Ahead?

The Extremes of the Demographic Continuum

In the early part of the 21st century, international population policy is no longer shaped by the macro-level issues of population growth and demographic trends. Rather, it has been reformulated with a nearly exclusive focus on gender equity and individual reproductive needs. The more holistic, humanistic approach that the 1994 Cairo conference has ushered in is laudable in improving the social position and health status of women worldwide. Yet the world faces demographic challenges that seem to have been cast aside in the process.

The countries of the world currently fall along a continuum of population growth that ranges from −0.6 percent per annum to over 4.0 percent. In this book we focus on two "clusters" along that continuum, which in fact make up the bulk of the world's population.

On one end are the vast majority of developing countries with fertility rates above replacement level. As we have seen in chapters 8 and 9, these countries run the gamut from those approaching replacement level to those with virtually no fertility decline. The decreases in fertility rates in many developing countries that began in the 1970s and have continued since then are promising signs that fertility desires do change in response to external factors, including better social conditions and increased availability of contraception. Many have heralded the drop in TFR from six to three children over the past 30–40 years as reason to believe that this trend will continue downward, thus solving the "demographic problem." Yet the final drop to replacement-level fertility promises to be particularly challenging. Indeed, governments worldwide are struggling to make services available to rural populations and other hard-to-reach groups. To do so—for both humanistic and demographic reasons—they need the sustained commitment of the international population community, including the donors.

On the other end of the demographic continuum is the small but historically important group of countries that have reached replacement-level fertility and have begun (or will soon begin) to experience negative population growth. To sustain their economies and ways of life, they must inevitably consider allowing greater immigration. Yet this brings with it a process of cultural adaptation that has not been easy for these countries in the past—to the limited extent it has occurred. In short, the cultural adaptations necessary for new groups to become assimilated into the majority populations constitute a major social challenge for the coming century.

Our message in writing this book is that on one hand, the international population community has dismissed its concern with demographic trends prematurely. On the other hand, it has yet to recognize and prepare for the inevitable cultural adaptations that will accompany immigration into receiving nations.

What Can We Expect in the 21st Century?

THE DEVELOPING WORLD

Around 1960, before fertility declines began to take place in the developing world, one could speak collectively of the developing world in terms of population growth rates: they were "high." In all three developing regions of the world, the TFR averaged around six children, and the natural increase was at least 2 percent per year (though there was evidence of an incipient fertility decline in Puerto Rico, Taiwan, South Korea, and the major cities of certain developing countries).

In the 21st century, demographic generalizations about developing countries no longer apply. Although no country in the developing world has achieved zero population growth, a number are at replacement-level fertility (and several have contraceptive prevalence rates higher than in the United States). These countries will continue to experience growth until the large number of "parents already born" have passed through their childbearing years at replacement-level fertility. Although this continued growth will provide some challenges to governments in terms of the educational, health, and other social services required by ever-larger numbers of people, the pace will slow and the numbers will remain manageable. Moreover, the quantity/quality trade-off that has produced lower fertility in these countries is also responsible for increased levels of education with each successive generation. The "Asian Tigers" illustrate the benefits that can accrue to nations that are simultaneously successful in improving economic conditions and lowering fertility.

At the other extreme are countries, many of which are in Africa, that show few signs of fertility decline. These countries will continue to grow at levels of 2–3 percent per year. Inevitably, continued growth will exert pressure on governments to provide social services and drain resources that could have been invested in human capital and infrastructure development. Yet the reality is that many of these countries are already overwhelmed by a host of other problems—political instability, civil unrest, natural disasters, lack of access to natural resources, inadequate governance, and lack of infrastructure, to name a few— that hinder their abilities to provide for the most basic needs of their populations. Moreover, governments that received support from the West during the Cold War have found much of that support withdrawn in the post–Cold War period, especially if they failed to demonstrate an interest in democratic governance. If these factors weren't enough, many of these same African nations are struggling to combat the effects of the AIDS epidemic and face unimaginable losses of the most productive members of their societies. Under such conditions, rapid population growth is yet one more contributor to the social and political ills of the countries with the highest fertility. In summary, curbing rapid population growth would not resolve the host of other problems facing many of these nations. At the same time, continued rapid population growth puts further pressures on existing systems that are counterproductive to efforts for sustained development.

In many countries, family planning was initially seen as something foreign that was "imported" to these countries from the (imperialistic) United States. However, the small-family norm has taken root with such force in many developing countries that even if support were withdrawn from subsidized family planning programs, a large percentage of current users would find alternative means of controlling their fertility.

The ability of nations to prosper in the 21st century depends on a host of factors, only one of which is the rate of population growth. Yet it is not coincidental that slowing population growth has gone hand in hand with improving the social conditions in developing countries around the world. Although there are exceptions (e.g., the oil-rich countries of the Middle East), we expect to see this pattern continue into the 21st century. A number of previously "developing countries" will increasingly resemble the developed world in terms of social conditions and quality of life. Still, slowing population growth will be extremely difficult in many of the world's poorest nations. The international community must continue to struggle to help these nations break the vicious cycle of poverty leading to high fertility that results in continued poverty and hinders development.

THE DEVELOPED WORLD

Low fertility in developed nations seems here to stay. Whereas demographic "predictions" are hazardous, the evolution in fertility rates over the past 30 years in developed nations provides strong evidence of a trend that is unlikely to reverse itself in the current social and economic climate.

This trend began in 1973, when a momentous new demographic phenomenon began to unfold throughout most of the developed world: fertility fell below the level of 2.1 births per woman needed to replace the population in the long run *and remained there.* Country after country—Canada, the then two Germanys, the United Kingdom, the United States—all reported fertility rates under two births per woman in 1983 and still lower rates in the early 1990s. Actual population size did not begin to fall immediately because all of the nations experienced a rise in their fertility rates after World War II—some for just a few years, others (such as Australia, Canada, and the United States) for

10 to 15 years. As a result, the number of young couples of childbearing ages was quite large in the 1970s, so that even with extraordinarily low fertility *per woman*, births continued to outnumber deaths each year, reflecting population *momentum*, discussed earlier.

But by the late 1970s, the effect of that momentum had subsided in many European countries, and in some, deaths began to outnumber births by the mid-1980s. Population decline was noted in Austria and East and West Germany. Continued immigration and the higher fertility of immigrants warded off decline for a time in other countries, but by the early 1980s, France and the United Kingdom were losing population, as was Hungary.

In the younger developed nations—the United States, Canada, Australia, New Zealand—the trend toward actual population decline will occur later than in Europe because of the reverberating impact of the tremendous post–World War II baby boom generation and because immigration levels have remained high. Nevertheless, the U.S. Census Bureau has projected that its population would stop growing at about 309 million by 2050 and then begin to decline, given continued below-replacement fertility and if net immigration was limited to 450,000 per year.[237]

Espenshade, Bouvier, and Arthur calculated that even with net immigration of 400,000 per year, the U.S. population would be reduced to 109 million before achieving zero growth in some 200 years, if the national fertility rate continued below replacement.[238]

This low fertility pattern, first noted some 20 years ago, continues to this date in most European countries as well as the United States, Canada, Australia, New Zealand, and Japan. According to the most recently published data, Italy, Spain, Romania, and the Czech Republic have fallen to 1.2 and below, the lowest in the world. Other nations in this group are not far behind. (See table 12.1 below.)

By 1995, Ireland (1.8 in 1998) and Portugal (1.4 in 1998) had joined the European low fertility groups and were accompanied by most of the new republics carved out of the erstwhile USSR. Thus, it is clear that fertility is remaining extremely low in all of Europe, Japan, and the former English colonies such as the United States, Canada, and Australia. It is also interesting to note that a slight increase in fertility has occurred in some Scandinavian countries. This may be a

COUNTRY	1970	1975	1982	1998
Europe				
Austria	2.3	1.8	1.7	1.4
Belgium	2.2	1.7	1.6	1.6
Denmark	2	1.9	1.4	1.8
France	2.5	1.9	1.9	1.7
Germany, East	2.2	1.5	1.9	-
Germany, West	2	1.5	1.4	1.3*
Hungary	2	2.4	1.8	1.4
Italy	2.4	2.2	1.6	1.2
Netherlands	2.6	1.7	1.5	1.5
Norway	2.5	2	1.7	1.8
Spain	2.9	2.8	2	1.2
Sweden	1.9	1.8	1.6	1.6
Switzerland	2.1	1.6	1.6	1.6
United Kingdom	2.4	1.8	1.8	1.7
Other Areas				
Australia	2.9	2.2	1.9	1.8
Canada	2.3	1.9	1.7	1.6
Japan	2.1	1.9	1.7	1.4
United States	2.5	1.8	1.9	2

Table 12.1—Total Fertility Rates in Selected Developed Countries, 1970, 1975, 1982, 1998

* This rate is for the combined Germanys.

Source: *World Population Data Sheets*, selected years (Washington, D.C.: Population Reference Bureau).

percursor of future trends and suggests that fertility could rise ever so slightly in other European countries in years to come.

Short-lived periods of low fertility have occurred in the past. During the Great Depression of the 1930s, fertility fell below replacement in most western European countries and in the United States. But the rates began to climb again by the late 1930s in the United States and during World War II in western Europe. Never before in modern history has fertility been so low in so many countries for such a long period as has been the case since 1973. And as of the late 1990s, the rates in most developed countries show little evidence of climbing back to the point where population growth, or at least population replacement, can be assured over the long run.

END OF GROWTH IN THE DEVELOPED WORLD

The significance of this new demographic pattern throughout most of the developed world suggests adaptation to a new era. The developed nations of the planet may well be poised on the brink of an entirely new age when the quantitative demands for labor will be modest, although the qualitative demands will be great.

We have seen harbingers of this momentous change. For example, John Naisbitt noted in his 1982 book, *Megatrends*: "In 1956 for the first time in American history, white-collar workers and technical-managerial positions outnumbered blue-collar workers. Industrial America was giving way to a new society where for the first time in history most of us worked with information rather than producing goods."[239] Naisbitt named this the "information society." Sociologist Daniel Bell called it the "postindustrial society."[240] These social observers, however, did not identify an end to population growth as an important ingredient in this emerging new society.

We are at the onset of a social upheaval as great as that touched off by the Industrial Revolution that began some 200 years ago. Interestingly, a demographic revolution occurred then also. With the improved living conditions resulting from the Industrial Revolution, mortality began to fall gradually from the end of the 18th century. Couples took a while to adjust to the fact that more of their children were surviving, so fertility generally did not begin to fall until late in the 19th century. During this interim period, population growth rose to over 1 percent a year in many western European countries, rates unprecedented in world history at that time. This growth helped supply workers needed for the cities' burgeoning industries, as well as immigrants to the "New World." Then western European couples realized that they could take advantage of improving social and economic opportunities by having fewer, but better educated, children. Today's population actors—at least those in developed nations—are once again responding appropriately to meet the needs of a new era.

This "information society," benefitting from high technology—and by 1990, from robotic technology and more recently from the Internet—will be knowledge-intensive rather than labor-intensive. The pattern of shifting the production of shoes and textiles, for example, to lower-wage developing countries is now being followed with the sophisticated "tools" of the information age. The 1983 decision by California-based Atari to move assembly-line work for its microcomputers to Hong Kong and Taiwan was but an early example of what has become standard practice. To some extent, that practice was behind the General Motors strike in 1998. The union argued that too many jobs were being sent to cheap labor countries such as Mexico. Even many service occupations may be eliminated in developed countries. Economist and Nobel prize winner Wassily Leontief has suggested that "the ability of the service sector to absorb displaced workers will diminish." He added, "As soon as not only the physical but also the controlling 'mental' functions involved in the production of goods and services can be performed without the participation of human labor, labor's role as an indispensable 'factor of production' will progressively diminish."[241]

THE LOGICAL RESULT: INCREASED INTERNATIONAL IMMIGRATION

The current and future demographic scenarios are increasingly shaped by the prospect of increased international migration. Perhaps more than at any time in the past, residents of the poorest nations are making the decision to move across international borders sometimes legally, sometimes illegally in search of a better life. Humans have always been peripatetic, but with the emergence of nation-states and political barriers in the late 19th and early 20th centuries, migration had become relatively controlled. However, with recent spectacular advances in communications and transportation facilities, added to the staggering poverty in developing nations (aggravated by rapid population growth), more and more people are ignoring these constraints and are moving despite the possibly dire consequences. This is happening all over the world, not only between developing and developed nations but also between the less affluent and more affluent developed countries, as from Portugal to France and Italy to Germany, and between the poorest developing countries and their somewhat better-off neighbors, as from Egypt to Saudi Arabia and Colombia to Venezuela.

In an earlier chapter we quoted the eminent American demographer, Kingsley Davis. He asked, "One wonders how long the inequalities of growth between the major regions can continue without an explosion?"[242] Davis's question is now being answered by millions upon millions of people who are giving up their long-accepted ways of life in search of something better. They may be legal immigrants whose decision to move resulted from considerable discussion and thought. They may be refugees forced to abandon their homeland because of political strife. They may be illegal immigrants who surreptitiously enter a country and lead guarded lives for fear of deportation.

It is evident that life in the 21st century will be greatly influenced by these three demographic phenomena: (1) the historically unprecedented levels of fertility decline in certain developed nations; (2) sustained population growth in the developing world over the past 40 years, which has created a "surplus population" in many nations; and (3) massive international migration by individuals in search of what they hope might be a better life.

Toward a New Society?

By the middle of the next century, the world's population will have surpassed 9 billion. We will have added about 3 billion since 2000. By then, however, the rate of growth will be a minimal 0.45 per 1,000. The human population will be approaching zero growth. Indeed, the more developed regions are projected to exhibit a negative growth rate of −0.23 compared to 0.56 for the less developed countries and 1.07 for the least developed countries.

Looking back from the year 2050, a demographer of that era may wonder, and perhaps laugh, as he or she discovers Orwell's fictional *1984*. Alas, George Orwell's fictional work, published in 1949 and read by tens of millions in 62 languages, will probably be little known by the middle of the next century. Perhaps this is because its portrayal of a totalitarian world in constant warfare by 1984 proved incorrect. Few people may recall that Orwell himself stated, "I do not believe that the kind of society I describe necessarily *will* arrive, but I believe (allowing, of course, for the fact that the book is a satire) that something resembling it *could* arrive."[243] However, another early 20th-century visionary, the great mathematician-philosopher Albert Einstein, did warn the people of this planet: "We shall require a substantially new manner of thinking if mankind is to survive."[244]

Perhaps as a result of Einstein's warnings, people in the middle of the 21st century may rediscover two other 20th-century authors whose works by then will be over a century old: the French philosopher Teilhard de Chardin and Lester Frank Ward, the father of American sociology and the first chair of the Sociology Department at Brown University.

Teilhard viewed evolution as an incomplete but ongoing process, with humankind always evolving, both mentally and socially, toward a final spiritual unity, a state he called "Noosphere." Ward felt that through the social sciences, humankind would move toward what he called "Sociocracy," where education would be the dynamic factor leading to a new type of social order.[245] Both argued eloquently for placing the good of society above that of the individual to the ultimate benefit of the latter. Teilhard's Noosphere and Ward's Sociocracy may be seriously considered among the intelligentsia of the next century as answers are sought for the problems faced at that time. Will this lead to new types of societies on this planet? Capitalism as it is known today and communism, which has already been discredited, may well disappear by 2050, and a new social democracy—a Sociocracy—could emerge where the good of the society comes first and individuals are the eventual beneficiaries.

Back in the 1970s and 1980s, and even today, some people expressed concern that the combination of rapid population growth in developing countries and below-replacement fertility in the developed countries would lead to the demise of Western capitalism. While the demographic scenario was correct, the concern was misplaced. Western capitalism played a vital role in the evolution of humankind on this planet, spawning the Industrial Revolution and the scientific and technological revolutions of the later 20th century. But after the tremendous changes that have transpired in the past 50 years, capitalism—or communism, for that matter—may no longer be appropriate given the scarcity of resources anticipated in the next century. The hoped-for renewed interest in Teilhard and Ward could mean the emergence of a whole new way of life, one that will be more rational, aiming toward zero population growth worldwide as soon as possible and toward increased international awareness and decreased national chauvinism—in a word, toward increased tolerance.

POINTS OF INTERVENTION

That planet Earth will continue to grow is not the question; how much we will allow it to grow is perhaps the most important issue facing humankind in the 21st century. In closing, we focus on the three demographic variables—fertility, mortality, and migration—and what actions are needed to improve our world in the 21st century.

FERTILITY

The noted anthropologist Margaret Meade expressed it best: "Every human society is faced with not one population problem but with two: how to beget and rear enough children and how not to beget and rear too many."[246] Those are situations facing two vastly different sections of the world today. Indeed, we have reason for optimism. Fertility rates have fallen in developing countries around the world, reflecting the desire for couples in those countries to have smaller families. Yet fertility remains high in a number of countries in Africa and (to a lesser extent) Latin America and Asia. Low levels of living combined with poor access to family planning services have sustained high fertility. Family planning programs must continue to make services available to potential clients through whatever mechanisms prove most feasible and culturally acceptable in the given setting. The integration of family planning with other reproductive health services (promoted at the Cairo conference) can be used to reach and attract new clients. But family planning must not get "lost" in the constellation of other services. Rather, it should remain a central pillar around which other reproductive health services are structured.

The Cairo conference focused on gender equity and empowerment of women as the pathway to lower fertility. We endorse this worldwide effort to improve the status of women, both for its own sake and for its potential contribution to fertility decline. Yet many who "bought into Cairo" seem to have stopped with women's empowerment and have discounted the long-term goals of population stabilization that were also part of the Cairo compromise.

The basic message of this book is that political stability, environmental integrity, and quality of life in both developed and developing countries depend on curbing population growth. The problems of continued growth should not be considered resolved simply because they were not highlighted in Cairo.

To this end, donor agencies must be willing to address this issue openly and explicitly. Governments need to clarify their objectives for family planning to include both improved health status for the individual users and enhanced welfare of the nation through diminished population growth. In terms of actual delivery of family planning services, programs must assure widespread access to services (multiple service facilities, including clinics, commercial outlets, and community-based distribution), and they should attract clients by providing quality, client-oriented services to meet individual needs. The increased constellation of services called for at the Cairo conference—and now in place in a growing number of countries—can further enhance the attractiveness of family planning to potential clients.

The hallmark of these services must be voluntarism, without which one violates the human rights of individuals. Some argue that change cannot take place quickly enough if we simply *wait* for couples to be ready for family planning. However, the experience of previously pronatalist countries in all three regions of the developing world is that couples *are ready* for smaller families, and the social norm for lower fertility can be achieved by making services widely available from competent client-oriented providers and by promoting these services through multiple communication channels. However, this scenario will be possible only if the international community maintains its commitment to the promotion of family planning and if donors provide the needed financial support to developing countries unable to fund the costs.

MORTALITY

All societies strive to reduce mortality in the name of self-preservation. Indeed, the rapid acceptance of "death control techniques"—in contrast to the slow uptake of birth control methods worldwide—largely explains the rapid population growth in the 20th century.

In this conclusion, we focus on one particular phenomenon: the AIDS epidemic in Africa. Despite the fact that lowering mortality results in more rapid population growth, there is a moral imperative to attempt to increase life expectancy and good health everywhere. The international population community must continue to support the efforts underway in Africa (and to a lesser extent elsewhere) to use existing family planning infrastructures (clinics, personnel, equipment) for the prevention of HIV/AIDS and the treatment of STDs that facilitate the transmission of AIDS.

MIGRATION

In the section on fertility above, we discuss population growth in the developing world. But what of the countries on the other end of the growth continuum—those facing negative growth? Certain European countries are already there; the newer developed nations—including the United States, Canada, Australia, and New Zealand—have below-replacement-level fertility. While this situation is welcome for a brief period, it cannot go on forever. We recognize that the total fertility rates may be somewhat misleading and may reflect a temporary postponement of births. If so, the TFRs will rise, albeit slightly. A second solution, should a nation's population fall too much, is to lower mortality. This is a worthwhile goal for all humans and should be emphasized everywhere. However, it is generally pursued for humanitarian, not demographic, reasons, and it is unclear how much further "progress" can be expected in that area. Under the circumstances, immigration seems inevitable, given that the countries with low fertility also hold economic advantages for potential immigrants. Problems of cultural assimilation and possible competition for numerical advantage may occur. The problems related to immigration will be manageable if the streams of immigrants remain small and newcomers are assimilated into the host society as rapidly as possible. Irredentism is not an option. Becoming German or American or Japanese is the only option for the newcomers, and the long-time residents of the receiving countries must be willing to accept this new phenomenon.

Yet the experience to date indicates that immigration is not always "controllable," especially in societies, such as the United States, that place a high priority on individual rights (and thus are unwilling to adopt measures for monitoring the population, such as national identification cards). Moreover, there is no guarantee that the new immigrant populations will wish to assimilate (for example, the Muslim populations in Europe have remained quite separate from the host country populations). However, this remains an ideal for the long-term political stability and cultural heritage of the receiving countries.

Whereas the issues of population growth and the fight against AIDS have brought countries together in pursuit of common solutions, this has occurred to a much lesser extent for international migration. The United Nations states that anyone has the right to move from his or her country of residence, but it does not state that all countries must accept newcomers. More international dialogue is needed on the social and political issues related to the inevitable increases in international immigration in the 21st century.

Looking Ahead to Cairo+10

As this book goes to press, meetings have been held in the Hague and in New York to review "Cairo+5." Although there has been no formal announcement regarding the date or venue of the next world population conference (which one would expect for 2004, if the historical pattern holds), it seems a virtual certainty that such an event will take place some 10 years post-Cairo. By 2004, the planet's population will be fast approaching 7 billion inhabitants. Shouldn't this conference deal specifically with the issues of population growth and demographic trends in a way that did not happen in Cairo? The pendulum has swung from the narrow focus on macro-level population trends (in the early days of family planning) to the more recent negation of the importance of demographic trends at the Cairo conference. It is now time to regain a balance in which there is recognition that lower fertility is a desirable goal that can be achieved through persistent efforts to promote voluntary family planning. Ideally, each country will seriously examine its population growth in relation to a host of economic and environmental factors with the aim of estimating its own "optimum population." However, unrelenting support of voluntary family planning by the international community remains an essential ingredient to fertility decline in the long term.

The demography textbooks treat stationary population growth as an "ideal" scenario that in fact does not exist in the real world. The thesis behind this book is that the global community should in fact aspire to this model. Population "stabilization" simply means achieving a constant level of growth, which could spell continued growth until the earth's population does reach its physical carrying capacity (the exact level of which remains in the realm of speculation). In the post-Cairo era, the discussion of demographic objectives is politically incorrect. Notwithstanding, the need to curb population growth remains urgent and the international population community has a responsibility to act.

Notes

Chapter 1: Introduction

1. United States, *World Population Prospects: The 1996 Revision* (New York: United Nations, 1998). Most of the data in this report are derived from an advance copy of this report. (*Author's note:* As we went to press, the advance copy of the tables from the UN 1998 revision of the world population projections was made available on the Internet at http://www.popin.org/pop1998/ [cited hereafter as the 1998 revisions]. Wherever appropriate, we will use these latest statistics, which take into account the AIDS pandemic in Africa and elsewhere.)

2. It is interesting to note that even a papal commission has recommended the two-child family, much to the dismay of the pope, who opposes even the advocacy of small families. He has condemned "propaganda and misinformation directed at persuading couples that they must limit their families to one or two children." Greg Burke, "Pope Warns UN Not to Try to Limit Family Size," Reuters, Vatican City, 18 March 1994.

3. Samuel P. Huntington, *The Clash of Civilizations and the Remaking of World Order* (New York: Simon and Shuster, 1997), 40–41. Huntington distinguishes between "civilization" and "civilizations" as follows: "A distinction exists between civilization in the singular and civilization in the plural. The idea of civilization was developed in the 18th century by French thinkers as the opposite of the concept 'barbarism.'. . . At the same time, however, people increasingly spoke of civilizations in the plural. This meant renunciation of a civilization defined as an ideal and a shift away from the assumption there was a single standard for what was civilized. . . . Instead there were many civilizations, each of which was civilized in its own way. . . . A civilization is a cultural entity.

4. Jean Raspail, *The Camp of Saints*, trans. (Petoskey, MI: Social Contract Press, 1998).

Chapter 2: A Brief History of Human Population

5. Joel Cohen, *How Many People Can the Earth Support?* (New York: W. W. Norton, 1995), 76.

6. "World Population: Will This Runaway Train Crush Us All?" *Los Angeles Times,* 25 December 1994, 2.

7. George F. Kennan, *At a Century's Ending* (New York: W. W. Norton, 1996), 10.

8. George F. Kennan, *Around the Cragged Hill: A Personal and Political Philosophy* (New York: W. W. Norton, 1993), 54.

9. This, of course, is a very brief description of the demographic transition model.

10. By age, we do not mean historical age. We are concerned with the average age of a nation's population. The median age is such a measure, as is the proportional distribution by five-year age groups.

11. These data are derived from the *1998 World Population Data Sheet* (Washington, D.C.: Population Reference Bureau, 1998).

12. Ansley J. Coale, "How a Population Ages or Grows Younger," in *Population: The Vital Revolution,* ed. Ronald Freedman (New York: Doubleday-Anchor, 1964), 37—47.

13. Actually, 35 percent of all Asians reside in China and another 27 percent live in India.

14. Huntington, *The Clash of Civilizations,* 117.

Chapter 3: World Population in the 21st Century

15. These differ from earlier long-term projections. Traditionally, these projections, whether "high," "medium," or "low," assumed that eventually all countries would reach replacement fertility. The only difference was the time it would take to reach that point. This optimistic assumption has long been a point of contention when UN projections are discussed.

16. The short-term projections from the United Nations have been released (*World Population Prospects: The 1992 Revision*). These data look at the population from 1992 to 2025. Generally, when examining that period of time, we will rely on this set of data rather than those cited earlier. Very slight differences are noted in the various projections. In the earlier long-term publication, the USSR is treated as a separate entity. In the latest publication, the former USSR is also considered separately. The Baltic states (Estonia, Latvia, and Lithuania) have been moved from the category of the former USSR to northern Europe. Since that release, a new revision has been made available, in part, on the Internet; however, the full report will not be available until mid-1999. Wherever possible, we rely on these newest projections obtained from the Internet.

17. Cohen, *How Many People,* 367.

18. Barbara Crossette, "'Oldest Old' 80 and Over Increasing Globally," *New York Times,* 22 December 1996, 12.

19. Nicholas Kristoff, "Aging World, New Wrinkles," *New York Times,* 22 September 1996, 1.

20. United Nations Development Program, *Human Development Report 1992* (New York: Oxford University Press, 1992), 54.

21. United Nations (UN) Population Fund, *The State of World Population 1993* (New York: United Nations, 1993), 9.

22. UN Population Fund, *The State of World Population 1993,* 6.

23. UN Population Fund, *The State of World Population 1993,* 9.

24. World Watch Institute, *State of the World 1990* (Washington: 1990), 42.

25. Paul Kennedy, *Preparing for the Twenty-First Century* (New York: Random House, 1993), 331.

26. Gina Kolata, "Model Shows How Improved Medical Care Allowed Population Surge," *New York Times,* 7 January 1997, B12.

27. Kennedy, *Preparing for the Twenty-first Century,* 277.

28. For a broad discussion of these findings, see Leon F. Bouvier and Lindsey Grant, *How Many Americans? Population, Immigration, and the Environment* (San Francisco: Sierra Club Books, 1994), chapter 1.

29. "Inequity, Population Growth Combine to Fuel Record Movement of People," press summary of *The State of World Population 1993,* 2.

30. Jonas Widgren, "International Migration and Regional Stability," *International Affairs* 66, no. 4 (1990): 750.

31. Michael S. Teitelbaum and Jay M. Winter, *The Fear of Population Decline* (New York: Academic Press, 1985), 126.

32. Kennedy, *Preparing for the Twenty-first Century,* 155.

33. Wayne Gibbons, "Immigration Reform in Australia: Recent Experiences," paper presented at the U.S. Department of Labor Conference, Washington, D.C., 19–20 September 1991.

34. Chatswood Journal, "Sea Change Down Under: Drifting to the Orient?" *New York Times,* 7 February 1997, 21.

35. Associated Press, "Australian Politician Blames Minorities," *Orlando Sentinel,* 11 May 1997, A-18.

36. As cited in William Drozniak, "Rolling up a Worn-Out Welcome Mat," *Washington Post,* 23 July 1993, 11.

37. Huntington, *The Clash of Civilizations,* 202.

38. See, for example, Thomas Muller, *Immigrants and the American City* (New York: New York University Press, 1993).

39. Bouvier and Grant, *How Many Americans?,* 77.

40. U.S. Bureau of the Census, *Current Population Reports*, P-25-1092, "Population Projections of the United States by Age, Sex, Race, and Hispanic Origin: 1992 to 2050" (Washington, D.C.: U.S. Government Printing Office, 1993), 62.

41. Bouvier and Grant, *How Many Americans?*, 120, table 4.4.

42. Linda Martin, "The Graying of Japan," *Population Bulletin* 44, no. 2 (July 1989): 36.

43. Japan Institute of Population Problems, *Population Projections for Japan: 1985–2025* (Tokyo: Ministry of Health and Welfare, 1987).

44. "Baby May Make 3, but in Japan That's Not Enough," *New York Times*, 6 October 1996, 3.

45. Gerhard Heilig, "Germany's Population: Turbulent Past, Uncertain Future," *Population Bulletin* 45, no. 4 (December 1990): 25–26. This entire section is derived from the Heilig report.

46. U.S. Bureau of the Census, *Current Population Reports*, xi.

47. Heilig, "Germany's Population," 33–34.

48. Kennedy, *Preparing for the Twenty-First Century*, 155.

49. T. Carrington, "Central Europe Borders Tighten as Emigres Flood in from East," *Wall Street Journal*, 8 February 1991, A8.

50. Kennedy, *Preparing for the Twenty-first Century*, 343.

51. Nicholas Eberstadt, cited in "German State Offers Cash to Encourage a Baby Boom," *Orlando Sentinel*, 27 November 1994, A-16.

52. Kennedy, *Preparing for the Twenty-first Century*, 343.

53. Vernon Scott, "Scott's World," UPI Hollywood, 17 April 1997. Scott was promoting a PBS documentary produced by Ben Wattenberg. Most of the quotes cited in this section are derived from Lindsey Grant, "The UN 1996 Population Projections," *NPG Forum*, December 1997.

54. Joseph Chamie, chief of the UN Population Division, interviewed by Barbara Crossette, reported in "World Is less Crowded than Expected, the UN Reports," *New York Times*, 17 November 1996.

Chapter 4: Immigration

55. Huntington, *The Clash of Civilizations*, 198.

56. Alfred North Whitehead, *Science and the Modern World* (New York: Macmillian, 1925), 297–98.

57. We concentrate on recent and current migration. For a discussion of earlier movements, see L. Bouvier, Henry Shrock, and Harry Henderson, "International Migration: Yesterday, Today, and Tomorrow," *Population Bulletin* 32, no. 4 (August 1979).

58. This section is based heavily on Sharon Russell and Michael Teitelbaum, *International Migration and International Trade* (Washington: World Bank, 1992), 67.

59. UN Population Fund, *The State of World Population 1993*, 10.

60. Fred Arnold et al., "Estimating the Immigration Multiplier: An Analysis of Recent Korean and Filipino Immigration to the U.S.," *International Migration Review* 23, no. 4 (1989): 813.

61. Huntington, *The Clash of Civilizations*, 198.

62. Huntington, *The Clash of Civilizations*, 202.

63. Much of this section is based on P. Martin and J. Widgren, "International Migration," *Population Bulletin* 51, no. 1 (April 1996).

64. United Nations, *World Population Prospects: The 1994 Revision* (New York: United Nations, 1995), 128.

65. Martin and Widgren, "International Migration," 6.

66. Russell and Teitelbaum, *International Migration and International Trade*, 1.

67. For example, it is estimated that some 5 million Chinese are living illegally in Siberia. In comparison, the Russian population of Eastern Siberia is about 7 million. Huntington, *The Clash of Civilization*, 243.

68. Japan, for example, has been successful in keeping out immigrants from other Asian countries. One might ask why the early 1990 exodus from China did not proceed to nearby Japan rather than the United States.

69. Such acceptance may not be as difficult as imagined. Consider the fact that the president of Peru, Alberto Fujimori, is of Japanese ancestry. Would anyone deny that he is a true Peruvian?

70. Huntington, *The Clash of Civilizations*, 204.

71. Michael Teitelbaum, "The Population Threat: Stemming Fertility Rates and Migration Flows," *Foreign Affairs* 74 (winter 1992–93): 63–78.

72. As cited in Bob Reiss, "The Melting Pot," *Potomac Magazine* (*Washington Post*), 17 July 1977, 27.

73. As cited in "Could There Be a Flood," *Social Contract* 8, no. 2 (January 1998): 91.

74. Kingsley Davis, *Human Society* (New York: Macmillan, 1948), 103.

75. Anthony Richmond, "Sociology of Migration in the Industrial and Post-Industrial Societies," in *International Migration: The Third World and the New World*, ed. A. Richmond and D. Kubat (London: Russell Sage, 1975), 238–82.

76. Davis, *Human Society*, 592.

77. As cited in Anthony Gottlieb's review of Lester Thurow's *The Future of Capitalism*, "Future Shock," *New York Times* book review, 31 March 1996, 9.

78. John Tanton, *The Ecologist* 6, no. 6 (July 1976): 23.

79. John Stuart Mill, *Principles of Political Economy with Some Applications to Social Philosophy*, 2 vols., ed. V. W. Bladen and J. M. Robson (Toronto: University of Toronto Press, 1848; London: Routledge and Kegan Paul, 1965), bk. 4, chap. 4, 756–57.

Chapter 5: The Three Demographic Billionaires: China, India, and the Muslim World

80. Huntington, *The Clash of Civilizations*, 88.
81. Huntington, *The Clash of Civilizations*, 111.
82. Huntington, *The Clash of Civilizations*, 117.
83. Huntington, *The Clash of Civilizations*, 119–20. Recall too the earlier quote attributed to the Prime Minister of Malaysia.

Chapter 6: Support for International Population Assistance

84. D. Hodgson and Susan Watkins, "Feminists and Neo-Malthusians: Past and Present Alliances," *Population and Development Review* 23, no. 3 (1997): 469–523.
85. John R. Weeks, *Population: An Introduction to Concepts and Issues* (Belmont, Calif.: Wadsworth, 1994), 61.
86. Hodgson and Watkins, "Feminists and Neo-Malthusians."
87. Hodgson and Watkins, "Feminists and Neo-Malthusians."
88. Later renamed the United Nations Population Fund.
89. Lori Ashford, "New Perspectives on Population: Lessons from Cairo," *Population Bulletin* 50, no. 1 (1995).
90. Hodgson and Watkins, "Feminists and Neo-Malthusians."
91. C. Alison McIntosh and Jason L. Finkle, "The Cairo Conference on Population and Development: A New Paradigm," *Population and Development Review* 21, no. 2 (1995): 223–60.
92. Hodgson and Watkins, "Feminists and Neo-Malthusians."
93. McIntosh and Finkle, "The Cairo Conference," 227.
94. Alaka M. Basu, "The New International Population Movement: A Framework for a Constructive Critique," *Health Transition Review* 7, Supplement 4 (1997): 7–31; and Harriet B. Presser, "Demography, Feminism, and the Science-Policy Nexus," *Population and Development Review* 23, no. 2 (1997): 295–331.
95. Steven W. Sinding, John A. Ross, and Allan G. Rosenfield, "Seeking Common Ground: Unmet Need and Demographic Goals," *International Family Planning Perspectives* 20, no. 1 (1994).
96. Sinding et al., "Seeking Common Ground."

97. Hodgson and Watkins, "Feminists and Neo-Malthusians."

98. Gregory H. Fox, "American Population Policy Abroad: The Mexico City Abortion Funding Restrictions," *Journal of International Law and Politics* (1986): 609–62.

99. Jason L. Finkle and C. Alison McIntosh (eds.), *The New Politics of Population: Conflict and Consensus in Family Planning* (New York: Population Council, 1994).

100. Planned Parenthood Federation of America, Inc., "International Family Planning: The Need for Services," PPFA website http://www.plannedparenthood.org/ - 1998.

101. "Why the Global Gag Rule Undermines U.S. Foreign Policy and Harms Women's Health," Population Action International, 1998.

102. "Factsheet: Why the United States Should Support UNFPA," Population Action International, 1998.

103. "International Population Assistance Update: Recent Trends in Donor Assistance," Population Action International, 1997.

104. "Issues in Brief: Endangered: U.S. Aid for Family Planning Overseas," Alan Gutmacher Institute, 1996.

105. "Legislative News and Views on Population," Population Action International, 3 July 1997.

106. "Issues in Brief: Endangered," Alan Gutmacher Institute.

107. "Legislative and Policy Update: Summary of Actions to Date," Population Action International, 28 February 1997.

108. "Legislative and Policy Update: Summary of Actions to Date," Population Action International, 21 November 1997.

109. "Legislative and Policy Update: Summary of Actions to Date," Population Action International, 21 November 1997.

110. John C. Caldwell, "Reaching a Stationary Global Population: What We Have Learnt, What We Must Do," *Health Transition Review* 7, Supplement 4 (1997): 37–42.

111. Working Group on Population Growth and Economic Development, Committee on Population, National Research Council, *Population Growth and Economic Development: Policy Questions* (Washington, D.C.: National Academy Press, 1986); and Hodgson and Watkins, "Feminists and Neo-Malthusians."

Chapter 7: Determinants of Contraceptive Use and Lower Fertility

112. Population Reference Bureau, "World Population Data Sheet," Washington D.C., 1998. Note: Malta and Slovenia report higher levels of

prevalence than China but are not recognized thusly in this text based on their small size and unknown quality of data.

113. The 1998 figures for South Asia include the following countries: Bangladesh, India, Iran, Pakistan, Sri Lanka, Kazakhstan, Uzbekistan, Bhutan, Nepal, and Afghanistan.

114. Population Reference Bureau, "World Population Data Sheet."

115. Population Reference Bureau, "World Population Data Sheet."

116. National Research Council, *Factors Affecting Contraceptive Use in Sub-Saharan Africa* (Washington, D.C.: Academic Press, 1993).

117. John C. Caldwell, "Reaching a Stationary Global Population," 37–42.

118. Rodolfo A. Bulatao, *The Value of Family Planning Programs in Developing Countries* (Santa Monica, Calif.: Rand, 1998).

119. "Factsheet: Why the United States Should Support UNFPA," Population Action International, 1998.

120. National Research Council, "Factors Affecting Contraceptive Use," 132.

121. National Research Council, "Factors Affecting Contraceptive Use."

122. Robert A. Hatcher, Ward Rinehart, Richard Blackburn, and Judith S. Geller, *The Essentials of Contraceptive Technology* (Baltimore, MD: Johns Hopkins University, Population Information Program, 1997).

123. Bulatao, *The Value of Family Planning Programs.*

124. John Bongaarts, "Population Policy Options in the Developing World," *Science* 263 (11 February 1994).

125. Shireen J. Jejeebhoy, *Women's Education, Autonomy, and Reproductive Behavior: Experience from Developing Countries* (Oxford: Clarendon Press, 1995).

126. Gary Becker and H. Lewis, "On the Interaction between the Quantity and Quality of Children," *Journal of Political Economy* 81, no. 2, part 2 (1973): 279–88; and Jack C. Caldwell, "Mass Education as a Determinant of Fertility Decline," chap. 10 in J. Caldwell, *Theory of Fertility Decline* (London: Academic Press, 1982).

127. National Research Council, "Factors Affecting Contraceptive Use."

128. Bongaarts, "Population Policy Options."

129. K. Chibalonza, C. Chirhamolekwa, and J. T. Bertrand, "Attitudes toward Tubal Ligation among Acceptors, Potential Candidates, and Husbands in Zaire," *Studies in Family Planning* 20 (1989): 273.

130. Population Reference Bureau, "World Population Data Sheet."

131. Instituto Nacional de Estadistica et al., "Encuesta Nacional de Salud Materno Infantil 1995," Guatemala City, 1996.

132. National Research Council, "Factors Affecting Contraceptive Use."

133. J. Cleland and W. Parker Mauldin, "The Promotion of Family Planning by Financial Payments: The Case of Bangladesh," *Studies in Family Planning* 22, no. 1 (1991): 1–18.

134. UNFPA, "The Role of Incentives in Family Planning Programmes: A Report of UNFPA/EWPI Technical Working Group Meeting on the Role of Incentives in Family Planning Programmes," Population Development Studies No. 4, East-West Center, Honolulu, Hawaii, 1980.

135. Lynn P. Freedman and Stephen L. Isaacs, "Human Rights and Reproductive Choice," *Studies in Family Planning* 24, no. 1 (1993): 18–30.

136. Stephen L. Isaacs, "Incentives, Population Policy, and Reproductive Rights: Ethical Issues," *Studies in Family Planning* 26, no. 6 (1995): 363–68.

137. Robert M. Veatch, "Governmental Population Incentives: Ethical Issues at Stake," *Studies in Family Planning* 8, no. 4 (1979): 100–108.

138. John B. Starr, *Understanding China: A Guide to China's Economy, History, and Political Structure* (New York: Hill and Wang, 1997).

139. J. Saloff and A. Wong, "Are Disincentives Coercive? The View from Singapore," *International Family Planning Perspectives* 4, no. 2 (1979): 50–55.

140. Malcolm Gillis, D. H. Perkins, M. Roemer, and D. R. Snodgrass, *Economics of Development*, 4th ed. (New York: W.W. Norton and Company, 1996).

141. Barbara Crossette, "How to Fix a Crowded World: Add People," *New York Times*, 2 November 1997.

142. Gillis et al., *Economics of Development.*

143. Isaacs, "Incentives, Population Policy, and Reproductive Rights."

144. Bongaarts, "Population Policy Options."

145. E. Croll, *Changing Identities of Chinese Women* (Hong Kong: Hong Kong University Press, 1995).

146. Michael Teitelbaum, "Fertility Effects of the Abolition of Legal Abortion in Romania," *Population Studies* 27, no. 3 (1972).

Chapter 8: Promoting Lower Fertility in the Post-Cairo Era

147. Alaka M. Basu, "The New International Population Movement: A Framework for a Constructive Critique," *Health Transition Review* 7, Supplement 4 (1997): 7–31; and Harriet B. Presser, "Demography, Feminism, and the Science-Policy Nexus," *Population and Development Review* 23, no. 2 (1997): 295–331.

148. Amy O. Tsui, "Reforming Population Paradigms for Science and Action," in *Curbing Population Growth: An Insider's Perspective on the Population Movement*, Oscar Harkavy (New York: Plenum Press, 1995).

149. United States Agency for International Development, "USAID's Strategy for Stabilizing World Population Growth and Protecting Human Health," *Population and Development Review* 20, no. 2 (June 1994).

150. Oscar Harkavy, *Curbing Population Growth: An Insider's Perspective on the Population Movement* (New York: Plenum Press, 1995).

151. Basu, "The New International Population Movement."

152. Basu, "The New International Population Movement."

153. Personal communication, Steven Sinding, 1998.

154. Sinding, et al., "Seeking Common Ground."

155. Julian Simon, *The Ultimate Resource* (Princeton: Princeton University Press, 1981).

156. Joel L. Swerdlow, "Population," *National Geographic* 4 (October 1998).

157. International Planned Parenthood Federation, "Vision 2000: Strategic Plan," IPPF Arab World Regional Office, Tunis, Tunisia, 1992.

158. Although this description was written based on a recent visit to Mexico by the second author, the Mexico case is also cited by Caldwell, "Reaching a Stationary Global Population," 37–42.

159. Consejo Nacional de Población (CONAPO)—The National Population Council; Secretaria de Salud (SSA) The Ministry of Health; Instituto Mexicano del Seguro Social (IMSS) Social Security Institute; Instituto de Seguridad y Servicios Sociales para los Trabajadores del Estado (ISSSTE) Social Security Institute for State Employees.

160. Fundación Mexicana para la Planeación Familiar, Asociación Civil, A.C. (MEXFAM)—Mexican Foundation for Family Planning, Civil Association; Federación Mexicana de Asociaciones Privadas de Salud y Desarrollo Comunitario, A.C. (FEMAP)-Mexican Federation of Private Health Associations and Community Development.

161. United Nations Population Division, *World Population Prospects: The 1998 Revision* (New York: United Nations, forthcoming 1999).

162. W. Cates and Katherine M. Stone, "Family Planning, Sexually Transmitted Diseases and Contraceptive Choice: A Literature Update Part I," *Family Planning Perspectives* 24, no. 2 (1992): 75–84.

163. Malcolm Potts, Roy Anderson, and Marie-Claude Boily, "Slowing the Spread of Human Immunodeficiency Virus in Developing Countries," *Lancet* 338 (1991): 608–13.

164. Potts, et al., "Slowing the Spread."

165. Maria De Bruyn, "Women and AIDS in Developing Countries," *Social Science and Medicine* 34, no. 3 (1992): 249–62.

166. Cates and Stone, "Family Planning."

167. Potts et al., "Slowing the Spread."

168. W. Cates, "Contraception, Unintended Pregnancies, and Sexually Transmitted Diseases: Why Isn't a Simple Solution Possible?" *American Journal of Epidemiology* 143, no. 4 (1996): 311–18.

169. Bongaarts, "Population Policy Options."

170. Paul T. Schultz, "Returns to Women's Education" in *Women's Education in Developing Countries: Barriers, Benefits, and Policies,* ed. Elizabeth King and M. Anne Hill (Baltimore: Johns Hopkins University Press, 1993); and John Cleland and German Rodriquez, "The Effect of Parental Education on Marital Fertility in Developing Countries," *Population Studies* 42, no. 3 (1988): 419–42.

171. John Knodel and Gavin W. Jones, "Post-Cairo Population Policy: Does Promoting Girls' Schooling Miss the Mark?" *Population and Development Review* 22, no. 4 (1996): 683–702.

172. Bryant Robey, Phyllis Tilson Piotrow, and Cynthia Salter, "Making Programs Work," *Population Reports* Series J, no. 40 (1994): 1–27; and Dennis A. Ahlburg and Ian Diamond, "Evaluating the Impact of Family Planning Programmes," in *The Impact of Population Growth on Well-Being in Developing Countries,* ed. Dennis A. Ahlburg, Allen C. Kelly, and Karen Oppenheim Mason (Berlin: Springer, 1996).

173. Robey et al., "Making Programs Work."

174. K. Hemmer, as quoted in Robey et al., "Making Programs Work."

175. M. Arends-Kuenning, B. Mensch, and M. R. Garate, "Comparing the Peru Service Availability Module and Situation Analysis," *Studies in Family Planning* 27, no. 1 (January/February 1996); and El-Zanaty and Associates, "Quality of Family Planning Services in Ministry of Health and Population Clinics Survey," National Population Council, Institutional Development Project, Research Management Unit, 1998.

176. J. D. Sherris, B. B. Ravenholt, R. Blackburn, R. H. Greenberg, N. Kak, and R. W. Porter, "Contraceptive Social Marketing : Lessons from Experience," *Population Reports,* Series J, no. 30, Baltimore, Johns Hopkins School of Public Health, Population Information Program (July–August 1985).

177. M. E. Gallen and W. Rinehart, "Operations Research: Lessons for Policy and Programs," *Population Reports,* Series J, no. 31, Baltimore, Johns Hopkins School of Public Health, Population Information Program (May–June 1986).

178. Phyllis T. Piotrow, D. Lawrence Kincaid, Jose G. Rimon II, and Ward Rinehart, *Health Communication: Lessons from Family Planning and Reproductive Health* (Westport, Conn.: Praeger, 1997).

179. Anrudh Jain, "Fertility Reduction and the Quality of Family Planning Services," *Studies in Family Planning* 20, no. 1 (1989): 1–16.

180. Michael Klitsch, "Still Waiting for the Contraceptive Revolution," *Family Planning Perspectives* 27, no. 6 (1995): 246–53.

181. Piotrow et al., *Health Communication*, cited above, provides a comprehensive overview of the use of communication campaigns to promote family planning and reproductive health.

182. Bulatao, *The Value of Family Planning Programs*.

183. Billings is a contraceptive method that involves observations of cervical secretions to identify the period of ovulation.

Chapter 9: Prescription for Action for the 21st Century

184. The total fertility rate (TFR) is defined as the average number of children a woman would have assuming that current age-specific birth rates remain constant throughout her childbearing years (usually considered to be ages 15 to 49).

185. The HIV seroprevalence rate is defined as the percentage of the population that is seropositive for HIV.

186. One limitation of this measure is that it uses data on urban population (only), whereas morbidity statistics relate to the national level. However, the data presented in the second section of this chapter (Distribution of Countries by Demographic Scenario) are based on models that do take into account seroprevalence in the rural population (where known) and/or the total population of the country that is urban.

187. Often-cited cases include the Rikai District study in Uganda and the Mwanza study in Tanzania as reported by M. Wawer et al., "Demographic Impact of HIV Infection in Rural Rikai District, Uganda: Results of a Population-Based Cohort Study," *AIDS* 8, no. 12 (December 1994):1707–13; and H. Grosskurth, F. Mosha, J. Todd, E. Mwijarubi, A. Klokke, K. Senkoro, et al., "Impact of Improved Treatment of Sexually Transmitted Diseases on HIV Infection in Rural Tanzania: Randomised Controlled Trial," Lancet 346 (1995): 530–36.

188. Instituto Nacional de Estadistica, et al. "Encuesta Nacional de Salud Materno Infantil 1995," Guatemala City, 1996.

189. Bureau of the Census.

190. Formerly Zaire.

191. Bureau of the Census.

192. Bongaarts, "Population Policy Options."

193. Although the Indian family planning program has had numerous problems over its 50-year history, it has contributed to fertility decline.

194. We make this distinction between successful family planning programs and strong socioeconomic conditions, recognizing that in many situa-

tions there is strong overlap between the two, which in fact is the set of conditions most conducive to increased contraceptive prevalence.

195. A. A. Popov, "Family Planning and Induced Abortion in the Post Soviet Russia of the Early 1990s: The Unmet Needs in Information Supply," Academy of Science of Russian Federation, Institute for Economic Forecasting, Centre of Demography and Human Ecology, August 1994, *Working Papers*, vol. 16; D. Pierotti, "Note from Estonia: From Abortion to Contraception," *Entre Nous* 25, no. 12 (May 1994); J. Friedman, F. Serbanescu, and C. Cruceanu, "Women in Need of Family Planning Services," Romania Reproductive Health Survey, 1993, published in collaboration with the Centers for Disease Control, Bucharest, Romania, IOMC, 1995; J. Pomfret, "Children? East European Women Say 'Not Now,'" *International Herald Tribune*, 14 February 1995, 1, 7.

196. National Research Council, *Factors Affecting Contraceptive Use in Sub-Saharan Africa* (Washington D.C.: Academic Press, 1993).

197. United Nations 1998 revision of the world population estimates and projections, United Nations website http://www.popin.org/pop1998/6.htm.

198. Population Reference Bureau, "World Population Data Sheet."

199. H. J. Page and R. Lesthaeghe, *Child-Spacing in Tropical Africa: Traditions and Change* (London: Academic Press, 1981).

200. John R. Weeks, "The Demography of Islamic Nations," *Population Bulletin* 42, no. 4 (December 1988).

201. Weeks, "The Demography of Islamic Nations."

202. J. A. Ross and W. Parker Mauldin, "Family Planning Programs: Efforts and Results, 1972–1994," *Studies in Family Planning* 27, no. 3 (1996): 147–143.

203. Ross and Mauldin, "Family Planning Programs."

204. J. Bruce, "Fundamental Elements of Quality of Care: A Simple Framework," *Studies in Family Planning* 21, no. 2 (1990): 61–90.

205. R. E. Lande and J. S. Geller, "Paying for Family Planning," Population Reports, Series J, no. 39, Baltimore, Johns Hopkins University, Population Information Program, November 1991.

206. Bulatao, *The Value of Family Planning Programs*.

207. Amy O. Tsui, Judith N. Wasserheit, and John G. Haaga, eds., *Reproductive Health in Developing Countries: Expanding Dimensions, Building Solutions* (Washington, D.C.: National Academy Press, 1997).

Chapter 10: Population Decline

208. Teitelbaum and Winter, *The Fear of Population Decline*. Much of this chapter is derived from this excellent monograph.

209. Technically, therefore, this is not really a rate since by definition, every "unit" in the denominator must be capable of performing the "act" (in this case, giving birth) in the numerator.

210. Interestingly, "be fruitful and multiply" was followed by "and replenish[ment of] the earth." Are we perhaps at that point now? At the "end of growth?"

211. Teitelbaum and Winter, *The Fear of Population Decline*, 2.

212. Jacques Chirac, "Jacques Chirac on French Population Issues," *Population and Development Review* 11 (1985), cited in Teitelbaum and Winter, *The Fear of Population Decline*, 123–24.

213. In Teitelbaum and Winter, *The Fear of Population Decline*, 39.

214. Arthur Newsholme, *The Declining Birth Rate: Its National and International Significance* (London: Cassell, 1906), 56–57.

215. D. Ferenczi, "La Politique economique mondiale et les changements dans la population," *Revue economique internationale* 2 (1934): 368.

216. Lincoln Day, *The Future of Low Birth-Rate Populations* (London: Routledge, 1992), 179.

217. Day, *The Future of Low Birth-Rate Populations*, 126.

218. Jennifer Cheesman Day, *Population Projections of the United States by Age, Sex, Race, and Hispanic Origin: 1995 to 2050*, U.S. Bureau of the Census, Current Population Reports, P–25–1130 (Washington, D.C.: Government Printing Office, 1996).

219. Edward O. Wilson, *Diversity of Life* (New York: W.W. Norton, 1993), 329.

220. "World Population Data Sheet," Population Reference Bureau, 1998.

221. Day, *The Future of Low Birth-Rate Populations*, 45.

222. For a detailed discussion of these issues, see Day, *The Future of Low Birth-Rate Populations*, especially chapters 3 and 4.

223. See Milton Gordon, *Assimilation in American Life* (New York: Oxford Press, 1964), chapter 3.

224. Leon Bouvier, *1988 Immigration: Diversity in the U.S.* (New York: Walker and Co., 1990), 34.

225. Cited in Willi Paul Adams, "A Dubious Host," *The Wilson Quarterly* (New York: New Years, 1924): 124.

226. Stanley Lieberson, "Unhyphenated Whites in the United States," in *Ethnicity and Race in the USA: Toward the 21st Century*, ed. Richard Alba (London: Routledge and Kegan Paul, 1985), 179.

227. Robert C. Christopher, *Crashing the Gates: The De-Wasping of America's Power Elite* (New York: Simon and Schuster, 1989), 17.

228. Kurt Vonnegut, *Bluebeard* (New York: Delacorte Press, 1987), 179.

229. Christopher, *Crashing the Gates*, 20.

230. Thomas J. Archdeacon, "Melting Pot or Cultural Pluralism? Changing Views on American Ethnicity," *Revue Europeene des Migrations Internationales* 6, no. 1 (1990): 18.

231. Theodore White, *America in Search of Itself: The Making of the President 1956–1980* (New York: Harper and Row, 1982), 367.

232. For a detailed discussion of pluralistic assimilation and cultural adaptation in the United States, see Leon F. Bouvier, *Peaceful Invasions: Immigration and Changing America* (Washington, D.C.: Center for Population Studies, 1992).

233. It is noteworthy that the success in the assimilation of Europeans occurred during a period when immigration to the United States was quite low (1921–1940). This gave the newcomers the time to adjust to their new surroundings.

234. T. S. Eliot, *Notes Toward the Definition of Culture* (New York: Harcourt, Brace, and Co., 1949), 49.

Chapter 11: The Stationary Population

235. Robert H. Weller and Leon F. Bouvier, *Population: Demography and Policy* (New York: St. Martin's Press, 1981), 337–38.

236. Thomas Espenshade, Leon Bouvier, and W. Bryan Arthur, "Immigration and the Stable Population Model," *Demography* 19, no. 1 (February 1982): 132.

Chapter 12: What Lies Ahead?

237. U.S. Bureau of the Census, "Projections of the Population of the United States: 1982 to 2050" (Advance Report), *Current Population Reports,* Series P–25, no. 922, 1982.

238. Espenshade et al., "Immigration and the Stable Population Model."

239. John Naisbitt, *Megatrends: Ten Directions Transforming Our Lives* (New York: Warner Books, 1982), 12.

240. Daniel Bell, *The End of Ideology* (New York: Crowell-Collier, 1961); see also Benjamin S. Kleinberg, *American Society in the Post-Industrial Age* (New York: Merrill, 1973).

241. Wassily Leontief, "Technological Advance, Economic Growth, and Income Distribution," *Population and Development Review* 9, no. 3 (September 1983): 403–11.

242. Kingsley Davis, *Human Society* (New York: MacMillan, 1948), 592.

243. Quoted in Paul Gray, "That Year Is Almost Here," *Time,* 28 November 1983, 56.

244. Cited in Michael Kernan, "Growing up with the Bomb," *Washington Post,* 20 November 1983, 56.

245. Teilhard de Chardin, *The Phenomenon of Man* (New York: Harper and Row, 1959, English translation of French original published in 1940); Lester Frank Ward, *Applied Sociology: A Treatise on the Conscious Improvement of Society* (New York: Arno, 1974, reprint of original published in 1906).

246. Margaret Meade, *Male and Female,* 2d ed. (London: Pelican, 1943), 210.

Index